FIRST BEGINNINGS
From the Creation to
The Mountain of the Prophets
&
From Adam and Eve
to Job and the Patriarchs

FIRST BEGINNINGS

From the Creation to
The Mountain of the Prophets

From Adam and Eve
to Job and the Patriarchs

From the Visions of
ANNE CATHERINE EMMERICH

Selected, Edited & Arranged
With Extensive New Translations from
the Original Notes of Clemens Brentano by
JAMES R. WETMORE

Volume 1 of 12
of the Series: *New Light on the*
Visions of Anne Catherine Emmerich

(With 24 Illustrations)

 Angelico Press

First published in the USA
by Angelico Press 2018
Revised Text, New Text, Translations,
and Layout © James R. Wetmore 2018

For information, address:
Angelico Press
169 Monitor St.
Brooklyn, NY 11222
angelicopress.com

ISBN 978-1-62138-360-4 (pbk)
ISBN 978-1-62138-361-1 (cloth)
ISBN 978-1-62138-362-8 (ebook)

Cover Image:
J. James Tissot (French, 1836–1902)
The Creation (detail)
Cover Design: Michael Schrauzer

CONTENTS

Preface

ANNE Catherine Emmerich was born on September 8, 1774, at Flamske, near Coesfeld, Germany. From early childhood she was blessed with the gift of spiritual sight and lived almost constantly in inner vision of scenes of the Old and New Testaments. As a child, her visions were mostly of pre-Christian events, but these grew less frequent with the passing years, and by the time she had become, at twenty-nine, an Augustinian nun at the Order's convent in Dülmen, Germany, her visions had become concerned primarily with the life of Jesus Christ, although they encompassed also the lives of many saints and other personages (some unknown as yet to history) as well as far-reaching insights into the creation, the fall, a mysterious mountain of the prophets, the spiritual hierarchies, paradise and purgatory, the heavenly Jerusalem, and much besides.

In the context of Anne Catherine's visions, and related conversations, much was said also of spiritual labors, described symbolically as work in the "nuptial house," the "inner chamber," the "garden," and the "vineyard." In this way many teachings on the inner life and prayer came forward, along with detailed accounts of healing work and journeys for "poor souls" in purgatory or in past epochs. Anne Catherine also showed considerable concern for the souls of those around her, especially her later amanuensis Clemens Brentano, in connection with his initial lack of faith.

Owing to difficult political circumstances, Anne Catherine's convent was disbanded on December 3, 1811, and one by one the nuns in residence were obliged to leave. Anne Catherine—already very ill—withdrew to a small room in a house in Dülmen. By November, 1812, her illness had grown so severe that she was permanently confined to bed. Shortly thereafter, on December 29, 1812, she received the stigmata, a manifesting of the wounds suffered by Christ on the cross, and the highest outward sign of inner union with him. Unable to assimilate any form of nourishment, for the rest of her life she was sustained almost exclusively by water and the eucharist.

As news spread that she bore the stigmata (which bled on Fridays), more and more people came to see her. For us, the most significant of these was Clemens Brentano, who first visited her on Thursday morning, September 24, 1818. He was so impressed by the radiance of her being that he decided to relocate nearby in order to record her visions. Anne Catherine had already had a presentiment that someone—whom she called "the pilgrim"— would one day come to preserve her revelations. The moment Clemens Brentano entered her room, she recognized him as this pilgrim.

Brentano, a novelist and Romantic poet then living in Berlin, was associated with leading members of the Romantic Movement in Germany. He settled his affairs and moved from Berlin to Dülmen early in 1819. Thereafter he visited Anne Catherine every morning, noting down briefly all she related to him. After writing out a full report at home, he returned later the same day to read it back to her. She would then often expand upon certain points, or, if necessary, correct details.

On July 29, 1820, Anne Catherine began to communicate visions concerning the day-by-day life of Jesus. These visions encompassed the better part of his ministry, and she was able to describe in extraordinary detail the places he visited, his miracles and healings, his teaching activity in the synagogues and elsewhere, and the people around him. She not only named and described many of these people with astonishing concreteness, but spoke also of their families, their occupations, and other intimate biographical details.

It seems clear that Anne Catherine was called to relate these day-by-day details of the life and ministry of Jesus, and that Clemens Brentano was called to record all she communicated of her visions. They worked together daily until her death on February 9, 1824, except for one period of six months, during which Brentano was away, and several shorter periods when, mainly due to illness, it was impossible for Anne Catherine to communicate her visions.

ENCOUNTERING the visions of Anne Catherine Emmerich can raise the question: how is it possible that this woman, who never left the German region in which she was born and had very little education, could describe in such detail not only the story of creation; heaven, hell, and purgatory; the fall of angels and humanity; the spiritual hierarchies and saints; the Promise and the Ark of the Covenant; the apocalypse; spiritual warfare; and the heavenly Jerusalem—but *also* the geography and topography of Palestine and the customs and habits of people living there at the time of Jesus Christ? To at least partially answer this, the researcher upon whose work the *chronological* aspects of this new edition is largely based, Dr. Robert Powell, undertook an exhaustive analysis of her work, gradually laying bare the historical reality underlying the life of Jesus (see "Chronology" below). But his work was not done in isolation, for others had earlier laid some groundwork.

For example the French priest Abbé Julien Gouyet of Paris, after reading an account of Anne Catherine's visions concerning the death of the Virgin Mary near Ephesus, traveled there and searched the region. On October 18, 1881, guided by various particulars in her account, he discovered the ruins of a small stone building on a mountain (Bulbul Dag, "Mount Nightingale") overlooking the Aegean Sea with a view across to the remains of the ancient city of Ephesus. Abbé Gouyet was convinced that this was the house described in Anne Catherine's visions as the dwelling of the Virgin Mary during the last years of her life. He was at first ridiculed, but several years later the ruins were independently rediscovered by two Lazarist missionaries who had undertaken a similar search on the basis of Anne Catherine's visions. They determined that the building had been a place of pilgrimage in earlier times for Christians descended from the church of Ephesus, the community referred to by St. John (Rev. 2:1–7). The building had been known in those days as Panaya Kapulu, the house of the Blessed Virgin, and was revered as the place where she had died. Traditionally, the date of her death, August 15, was the *very day* of the annual pilgrimage to Panaya Kapulu.

That Anne Catherine's visions provide spiritual nourishment had long been the experience of many spiritual seekers, but the discovery of Panaya Kapulu confirmed that her visions could also (at least in part) be corroborated along conventional lines of research.

Sources

THE visions of Anne Catherine Emmerich have been published in English translation in various editions since late in the nineteenth century. These editions focused primarily on the visions of the life of Jesus Christ and of Mary, with some material drawn from Old Testament times also. However the *original* notes of Clemens Brentano contained material on many other fascinating subjects. Much of this material has not been readily available before now, either in German or in English translation, a gap that this twelve-volume *New Light on the Visions Anne Catherine Emmerich* series is meant at least to begin filling.

Until now the only translations available of some of this latter material appeared in the two-volume biography of Anne Catherine by Rev. Carl E. Schmöger, first published in English in 1885. Rev. Schmöger, who was also instrumental in the selection and arrangement of the visions related to the life of Jesus Christ upon which later English translations were based, included in the biography a selection of the supplemental material mentioned above —but his selection was necessarily limited.

Clemens Brentano himself was only able to compile from his notes a few volumes for publication, and upon his death the notes passed to his brother Christian, who had been an interested participant in Clemens's work with Anne Catherine from the start (in fact, Christian had arranged his brother's first meeting with the visionary). Christian, however, proved unable to coordinate the notes any further. And so the first phase of this seemingly insurmountable task fell in due course to Rev. Schmöger.

Then, in the last decades of the twentieth century, the German publisher Kohlhammer commenced publishing, under the auspices of the *Frankfurter Brentano Ausgabe*, an intended complete edition of Brentano's works, projected to number as many as sixty volumes. Part of this project was the publication of facsimiles of the thirty-eight notebooks of Brentano's notes of the visions of Anne Catherine. (Brentano also noted down details of their conversations in other contexts, as well as his own experiences while attending her.) With the Kohlhammer edition, a wider public would finally gain access to the originals upon which later compilations and translations of the visions had been based. However, this noble project has not been completed, and at present there is no indication whether it will recommence. An additional impediment for researchers in dealing with the facsimiles is the fact that Brentano's notes were penned in a now archaic German script that only specialists can read.

Thus matters stood until Jozef De Raedemaeker, a dedicated Belgian researcher, undertook the enormous task of transcribing the full body of notes from the archaic script into modern German—making it available in printed and digital form in 2009. The combined 38 notebooks exceed 7,300 pages and include many hand-drawn illustrations as well as typographic conventions to identify the contributions of others present at Anne Catherine's bedside, who sometimes took notes or added comments, and sometimes drawings.

ANYONE who does even minimal research on the visions of Anne Catherine Emmerich as depicted in the works attributed to Brentano's notes will soon discover that there are conflicting opinions regarding their fidelity to the words of Anne Catherine herself. This would be a subject in itself, but some remarks may be offered here. First, Anne Catherine, who had little formal education, spoke in a Low-German dialect that even Brentano, at the outset, had some difficulty understanding. Secondly, the material that was eventually fit together into a connected account in the published versions often represents a collation of as many as a dozen or more passages gleaned from visions separated sometimes by months, or even years. This can be partially explained by the fact that the visions were often related to events in the ecclesiastical year, to feasts of saints, to individuals with specific needs or requests, or to the presence of relics.

And so a great deal of work had to be done to organize and knit together related segments of visions, and to then arrange them in a meaningful sequence. Then again, it was deemed necessary to refine the language sufficiently to render it in a more contemporary idiom. There is, then, a legitimate concern that so famous and gifted a literary figure as Clemens Brentano might, even if unintentionally, have introduced some of his own impressions, interpretations, and sensitivities into his renditions. And a similar concern could be raised concerning Rev. Schmöger's subsequent arrangements, as well as those of later editors and translators working at yet a further remove.

Much of the debate on this subject, however, took place without ready access to the original notes, a defect that has now been remedied. At certain points in his transcriptions De Raedemaeker addresses this issue by comparing fragments of the original notes with versions of these same fragments as they appear in Rev. Schmöger's edition, after he in turn had worked, in some instances, with Brentano's own compilations from his original notes—and in some cases there are non-trivial discrepancies. This is an area that requires further research.

Perhaps I myself may be permitted to chime in here, as there are not many who have entered into this vast field, and I can at least appeal to many years of engagement with the visions of Anne Catherine, *including* examining De Raedemaeker's transcriptions of all thirty-eight notebooks. While thus occupied, I inevitably began to identify for myself many of the original sources upon which Rev. Schmöger based his versions well over a century ago, and in such cases could assess the fidelity of the latter to the former. Although such details do not lie within the scope of this series, I can say that, with very rare exceptions—especially allowing for the frequent need to splice together disparate fragments—Rev. Schmöger's renderings remain remarkably true to the original, and any minimal divergences are for the most part quite trivial, insofar as I have been able to investigate.

During this process, however, I *was* struck by the fact that considerable material had been *omitted*. This may well have been owing to the enormity of the task, as also to pagination limits set by the publisher; or also, partly a measure of Rev. Schmöger's personal judgment and concerns. Perhaps some of the excluded material seemed unintelligible to him, or even scandalous. However that may be, in this current series as much as possible of this neglected material has been extracted, translated, and incorporated in the relevant volumes.

It needs to be said also, in response to assertions (made mostly without benefit of access to his actual notes) that Brentano misrepresented Anne Catherine, or, even worse, took advantage of his notes to compile an independent literary work that might embellish his reputation, that in fact, in his notes, Brentano *candidly* reports *exactly* what he heard Anne Catherine say, *no matter* how extraordinary, puzzling, or even apparently contradictory. He himself offers many instances where only later—sometimes years after Anne Catherine had died—he (often with the help of academic experts) finally began to understand previously incomprehensible passages in the visions. He steadfastly refused—according to his own account and that of others—to edit out "difficulties," feeling himself, rather, under a sacred obligation to preserve his record intact and unaltered for posterity. And when the notes passed to his brother Christian, the latter adhered to the same policy.

Even without the benefit of access to the original notes on the part of most researchers, and even in face of an undercurrent of scepticism as to the authenticity of the visions, it may be worthwhile, in drawing this matter to a close for our present purposes, to note that on October 3, 2004, Anne Catherine was beatified by Pope John Paul II, who remarked: "Her example opened the hearts of poor and rich alike, of simple and cultured persons, whom she instructed in loving dedication to Jesus Christ." And in the Vatican's biography of Anne Catherine we read: "Her words, which have reached innumerable people in many languages from her modest room in Dülmen through the writings of Clemens Brentano are an outstanding proclamation of the gospel in service to salvation right up to the present day."

Chronology

PERHAPS the most surprising feature of this new series on Anne Catherine Emmerich will be the inclusion of *historical dates*—and so a brief discussion of this feature is offered below.

As described earlier, Anne Catherine was so attuned to the life of Jesus Christ as a mystical-historical reality that her comprehensive visions encompassed even minute details of time and place—testable "coordinates" in fact. This degree of precision was made possible by the many temporal as well as geographical descriptions and references contained in the visions—as mentioned earlier in connection with the discovery of the house of the Blessed Virgin.

Many chronologies of the life of Jesus Christ have been put forward over the centuries, but the dates offered in this current series differ from previous efforts in that they derive from the application of modern chronological and astro-chronological science to the whole of Anne Catherine's visions—which latter constitute a vast body of data internally consistent as to time and place to an extraordinary degree, so that, taking the generally agreed upon time period of Jesus's life, results of a high degree of reliability can be determined.

Naturally, the overriding value of the visions lies in the additional insight they offer into the life of Jesus Christ, so that for some the dating may represent no more than a convenient framework for study and meditation. Such readers need not trouble themselves about the specific dates, although they may nonetheless find that the chronology offers a useful way to maintain their orientation within any given volume, as also when referring to events in volumes already read. Some, however, will wish to assess for themselves the method by which specific dates have been thought reliable enough to include here. They may read elsewhere[1] the story of the determination of the chronology of the life of Jesus Christ included in these volumes.

---

[1] *The Visions of Anne Catherine Emmerich*, Book III, Appendix I (Kettering, OH: Angelico Press, 2015), which is based on the work of Dr. Robert Powell.

The New Light on the Visions
of Anne Catherine Emmerich *Series*

THE present book is one of the twelve volumes of the "New Light on the Visions of Anne Catherine Emmerich" series published by Angelico Press. This series supplements two earlier Angelico publications: *The Visions of Anne Catherine Emmerich*, Books I–III (1,700 pages in large format, with 600 illustrations and forty-three maps); and the smaller-format, slightly abridged edition: *Life, Passion, Death, & Resurrection of Jesus Christ* (*A Chronicle from the Visions of Anne Catherine Emmerich*), Books I–IV (1,770 pages with 150 illustrations and 43 maps). As described earlier, in 2009 Clemens Brentano's original notes of Anne Catherine's visions became readily available for reference. At that time the above texts were already nearing completion. With the appearance of these notes, however, the editor resolved to pause, and, to the extent possible, research this vast body of notes to ascertain what further light they might shed on what had by then been prepared for publication. While the better part of another decade was devoted to the task, much research, of course, remains to be done (see "Future Prospects" below). But at some point one must call a halt, and so, after the insertion of relevant new translations into the two sets mentioned above and their publication in 2015–2016, the present series was conceived as a means to present in various contexts such new material as has since then been selected and translated from the notes.

In general, the content of each volume of this series consists (1) of material selected by individual or theme from earlier translations—reviewed, supplemented, and revised where necessary, especially for consistency of usage; and (2) of newly selected and translated material germane to the content of that volume. With regard to both individuals and themes, the procedure was to extract every reference thus far located in the notes and in prior translations and weave them together into a connected account. The reader can thus find in one place almost all of what Anne Catherine had to say about any given individual or theme.

Virtually every individual in the biblical visions (approximately 250 in total) is referenced in the five *People of the New Testament* volumes (which include also some figures from earlier and later times). A separate volume, *The Life of the Virgin Mary*, is dedicated to Mary and her ancestry (including much on the Essenes); and another volume, *Scenes from the Lives of the Saints*, treats of fifty-nine saints. Separate volumes cover events prior to the appearance of the holy family: *First Beginnings* and *Mysteries of the Old Testament*. Two further volumes cover a multitude of separate themes: *Inner Life and Worlds of Soul & Spirit* and *Spiritual Works and Journeys*. A final volume represents a condensed, edited, rearranged, supplemented, and retypeset edition of Rev. Carl E. Schmöger's exhaustive biography of Anne Catherine, first published in English in 1885. For clarity of organization, much of this biography in its original form has been redistributed among other volumes of this series. What remains has also been enriched with newly-translated material. A list of all twelve volumes of this series appears at the conclusion of this preface.

Practical Considerations

IN view of the sometimes extensive wealth of material presented concerning certain individuals—especially major characters—a judicious essentializing of scenes has sometimes been resorted to. In some cases, especially those of closely related apostles and disciples (or others regularly treated together in the visions), rather than duplicating material, the expedient adopted was to disentangle scenes to the extent possible, so that the full story could be garnered gradually by reading the separate accounts of each. Nonetheless, since readers may jump around in their selection of individuals to study, some repetition was unavoidable in order to provide enough context to keep the separate accounts reasonably sequential and unified. Put another way, these volumes are conceived primarily as reference works to which one turns for particulars on specific persons or themes rather than as connected narratives to be read cover to cover. Of course, the volumes may be read in the latter fashion also, in which case the occasional repeated material will be more noticeable.

Another consideration was that some individuals play so great a role in the visions (e.g., John the Baptist, St. Joseph, Peter, Matthew, Judas, and the Virgin Mary) that it would be impractical to include every mention in a chronological itinerary. Emphasis in such cases has been placed primarily on more general and newly-translated material. Inquisitive readers can of course turn to the index of the large-format, three-volume *The Visions of Anne Catherine Emmerich* to expand their research on such individuals.

It must be well understood that all the editor could do was work with what Anne Catherine actually said. Some little-known (or even totally unknown) individuals may enjoy longer accounts in these volumes than other, very well known, figures from the gospels or later Christian tradition! There can be no question of assigning relative importance to any individual based solely upon how extensive Anne Catherine's visions of that person may have been. Likewise, stories may have gaps, or sometimes end abruptly. It is indeed unfortunate that (as Brentano repeatedly laments in his notes) so much was lost owing to Anne Catherine's considerable suffering, household distractions, and the many obligations laid upon her—all of which interfered with her visions and her capacity to recall them. And yet withal, how much we have to be grateful for!

To streamline as far as possible a complex text, these usages were established: The voice of the narrator (Rev. Schmöger) is put in italics. Direct citations from Brentano (and a few others) are put in quotes. Anne Catherine's text bears no quotation indicators *except* where references to her words are embedded in the two contexts just mentioned. Parentheses enclose supplemental material from Anne Catherine or Brentano; brackets enclose material from Rev. Schmöger or the present editor. Footnotes from the hand of Brentano are followed by CB; those consisting of further visionary content from Anne Catherine are—for clarity in this context—enclosed in quotation marks; all other unattributed footnotes have been supplied by the present editor, sometimes incorporating what seemed worth retaining from notes by others in earlier editions.[1]

---

[1] The most useful material of this sort has been integrated from notes to a version of *The Life of the Virgin Mary* provided by Rev. Sebastian Bullough, O.P., to whom we express our gratitude.

For convenience, especially in itineraries of individuals, dates are incorporated in what is otherwise purely Anne Catherine's visionary text. It must, however, be well understood that these dates are derivative, as mentioned in "Chronology" above, *not* from the hand of Anne Catherine. As another help, for many major figures, summaries are provided at the outset. These are often in the third person—as they represent a condensation by the editor—but are nonetheless derived directly from the visions.

In such a context as these visions represent, capitalization (a topic upon which there are many and various usages, and often passionate opinions) represented a particular challenge. In the end, after experimenting with progressively increasing degrees of simplification, it was determined—in order not to overly fatigue the reader of what essentially amounts to an extended narrative rather than devotional reading properly speaking—to implement a very spare policy indeed, reserving capitalization to the Deity, and to certain terms that in Anne Catherine's visions assume a unique significance, such as the Ark of the Covenant, and what she calls the Promise, or sometimes the Holy Thing, the Mystery or Sacrament (in this special sense), or even the Germ or Seed. Finally, in cases where more general considerations are followed by chronological extracts forming a connected itinerary, the break is signaled by a row of five typographic crosses.

Prospects for the Future

AS editor of this series I am only too aware of my limitations in the face of the awe-inspiring magnitude of the task. My initial inspiration was solely the *spiritual value* of Anne Catherine's visions as a means to help seekers find their way *back* to a faithful connection with Jesus Christ; or, in the case of so many in our time, find their way *for the first time* to a dawning awareness of what they may thus far have failed to see. Further, there are great, resonant depths in the visions, like choirs of symbolism. As time went on I could only go deeper, entering upon the work that has led now, finally, to completing this series. Along with spiritual benefits and guidance, it was and will ever remain also a thrilling journey of discovery. Now, with Brentano's original notes available thanks to the efforts of Jozef De Raedemaeker, there are further depths to explore, as alas—despite so many years of work—the rich sod has only been broken.

In the visions will be found fascinating indications and hints for archeologists, historians, linguists, theologians, students of comparative religion, chronologists, specialists in symbolism, and more. Over and above the *primary element* of spiritual inspiration, it is my hope that such specialists may in due course take up these visions (including the entire corpus of Brentano's notes) and press further forward. How one would love to see a foundation, a university, a religious sodality, or some private individual or group sponsor so important and propitious a project. If the largely solitary results presented here serve to advance such future research, if hearts and souls are moved and enriched by *The Anne Catherine Emmerich Series* as a whole, the effort will have achieved its primary purpose.

JAMES RICHARD WETMORE

Acknowledgments

IT is difficult to sift out elements from earlier translators of these visions, but our main debt of gratitude for much of the English text taken as a foundation in the current work is owed to Sir Michael Palairet. Incalculable thanks are owed to Jozef De Raedemaeker for his past and present work with the original handwritten notes of Clemens Brentano. Occasional assistance with translation was received from Mado Spiegler, James Morgante, and especially Harrie Salman. A special thanks goes to Robert Powell, who has been a companion at every stage of this journey owing to his dedication to Anne Catherine in every respect: researching, translating when necessary, and, preeminently, applying his skills to the task of establishing the chronology that has been incorporated in this edition (in which connection Fr. Helmut Fahsel should also be mentioned). Most line drawings in the volumes are taken from Brentano's notes; the occasional paintings included are from the hand of James J. Tissot, as are all but one of the cover illustrations.

The New Light on the Visions
of Anne Catherine Emmerich Series

First Beginnings

Adam and Eve Driven from Paradise

From the Creation to
the Mountain of the Prophets

Fall of the Angels

I SAW spreading out before me a boundless, resplendent space, above which floated a globe of light shining like a sun. I felt that it was the Unity of the Trinity. In my own mind, I named it the ONE VOICE, and I watched it producing its effects. Below the globe of light arose concentric circles of radiant choirs of spirits, wondrously bright and strong and beautiful. This second world of light floated like a sun under that higher sun.

These choirs came forth from the higher sun, as if born of love. Suddenly I saw some of them pause, rapt in the contemplation of their own beauty. They took complacency in self, they sought the highest beauty in self, they thought but of self, they existed but in self. At first all were lost in contemplation out of self, but soon some of them rested in self. At that instant, I saw this part of the glittering choirs hurled down, their beauty sunk in darkness, while the others, thronging quickly together, filled up their vacant places. And now the good angels occupied a smaller space. I did not see them leaving their places to pursue and combat the fallen choirs. The bad angels rested in self and fell away, while those that did not follow their example thronged into their vacant places. All this was instantaneous.

Then rising from below, I saw a dark disc, the future abode of the fallen spirits. I saw that they took possession of it against their will. It was much smaller than the sphere from which they had fallen, and they appeared to me to be closely crowded together.

I saw how from the dark disc the evil spirits streamed one after the other toward the earth. Yes, I saw the fall of the angels in my childhood and ever after, day and night, I dreaded their influence. I thought they must do great harm to the earth, for they are always around it. And I felt things would worsen. In all this there was something like the swarming of ants. They had grown, in truth, far darker and more hateful than they had appeared when first they fell.[1]

I saw the fallen angels in a much smaller, dark sphere in the depths. They were pressed much closer together than is the case in the heavenly choirs. Those already fallen into hell will never escape. But there remains a great company of evil spirits that inhabit an intermediary sphere, and upon the earth—passing ever and again into, and out of, hell. It is well they have no bodies, else they would obscure the light of the sun. We should see them floating around us like shadows.

Immediately after the fall, I saw the spirits in the shining circles humbling themselves before God. They did homage to Him and implored pardon for the fallen angels. At that moment I saw a movement in the luminous sphere in which God dwelt. Until then it had been motionless and, as I felt, awaiting that prayer.

---

[1] "As I beheld this, one of them rushed up quite close to me, and directed at me a most insulting barrage of words, asking what I thought I was doing, causing him such trouble! His wish was to break my neck, or so disgrace me as to bring me to ruin. Just wait, he said, and soon I shall marshall all your friends against you. Throughout, I thought only of God, and that he would nonetheless stand by me—and so did the fiend grow ever more enraged as I made clear to him that I was already well familiar with his various wiles. He was not large. His face had a human form, and though it bore no obvious grimace, yet was it inexpressibly horrible. Like all such spirits, it bore a darkly human form, ever in uneasy motion and as quick as the wind, twitching and stamping about. When finally he was gone, I saw myself on the earth and saw particular evil spirits moving through the air toward this or that great city or region. Above certain places, however, I saw spirits of great beauty driving away the evil ones—who then turned and flew on to some other place. I received an instruction that these beings were driven away through intercession; those who turned them aside had power over them, and it was they who permitted them whatever latitude was allowed. I saw perhaps four cities in which much evil held sway, and I had to laugh, as I saw larger, and quite elegant spirits draw near them. I thought to myself, 'Look, the great lords [cities] have also their great devils,' for they were, each of them, different in quality and function. Wherever they forced an entrance, I saw much congregating and confusion. Then, as I saw a great multitude of these evil spirits falling down, I thought that they must be on their way to as yet undiscovered lands."

After that action on the part of the angelic choirs, I felt assured that they would remain steadfast, that they would never fall away. It was made known to me that God in His Judgment, in His Eternal Sentence against the rebel angels, decreed the reign of strife until their vacant thrones are filled. But to fill those thrones seemed to me almost impossible, for it would take so long. The strife will, however, be upon the earth. There will be no strife above, for God has so ordained.

After I had received this assurance, I could no longer sympathize with Lucifer, for I saw that he had cast himself down by his own free, wicked will. Neither could I feel such anger against Adam. On the contrary, I felt great sympathy for him because I thought: It has been thus ordained.

Humankind was created to fill the choirs of the fallen angels. Were it not for the fall of Adam, humankind would have increased only till the number of the fallen angels was reached; and then the world would have come to an end. Had Adam and Eve lived to see even one sinless generation, they would not have fallen. I am certain that the world will last until the number of the fallen angels has been filled, until the wheat shall have been reaped from the chaff. Once I had a great and connected vision of sin and the whole plan of redemption. I saw all mysteries clearly and distinctly, but it is impossible for me to put all into words. I saw sin in its innumerable ramifications from the fall of the angels, and from Adam's fall, down to the present day, and I saw all the preparations for the repairing and redeeming down to the coming and death of Jesus. Jesus showed me the extraordinary blending, the intrinsic uncleanness of all creatures, as well as all that he had done from the very beginning for their purification and restoration. At the fall of the angels, myriads of bad spirits descended to earth and into the air. I saw many creatures under the influence of their wrath, possessed by them in many ways.

Formation of the Earth

IMMEDIATELY after the prayer of the faithful choirs and that movement in the Godhead, I saw below me, not far from and to the right of the world of shadows, another dark globe arise. I fixed my eyes steadily upon it. I beheld it as if in movement, growing larger and larger, as it were, bright spots breaking out upon it and encircling it like luminous bands. Here and there, they stretched out into brighter, broader plains, and at that moment I saw the form of the land setting boundaries to the water. In the bright places I saw a movement as of life, and on the land I beheld vegetation springing forth and myriads of living things arising. Child that I was, I fancied the plants were moving about.

Up to this moment, there was only a gray light like the sunrise, like early morning breaking over the earth, like nature awakening from sleep. And now all other parts of the picture faded. The sky became blue, the sun burst forth, but I saw only one part of the earth lighted up and shining. That spot was charming, glorious, and I thought: There is paradise!

Paradise

WHILE these changes were going on upon the dark globe, I saw, as it were, a streaming forth of light out of that highest of all the spheres, the God-sphere—that sphere in which God dwelt. It was as if the sun rose higher in the heavens, as if bright morning were awakening. It was the first morning. No created being had any knowledge of it, and it seemed as if all those created things had been there forever in their unsullied innocence. As the sun rose higher, I saw the plants and trees growing larger and larger. The waters became clearer and holier, colors grew purer and brighter —all was unspeakably charming. Creation was not then as it is now. Plants and flowers and trees had other forms. They are wild and misshapen now compared with what they were, for all things are now thoroughly degenerate.

When looking at the plants and fruits of our gardens—apricots for instance, which in southern climes are, as I have seen, so different from ours, so large, magnificent, and delicious—I often think: as miserable as are our fruits compared with those of the South, are the latter when compared with the fruits of paradise. I saw there roses, white and red, and I thought them symbols of Christ's passion and our redemption. I saw also palm trees and others, high and spreading, which cast their branches afar, as if forming roofs. Before the sun appeared, earthly things were puny; but in his beams they gradually increased in size, until they attained full growth.

The trees did not stand close together. Of all plants, at least of the largest, I saw only one of each kind, and they stood apart like seedlings set out in a garden bed. Vegetation was luxuriant, perfectly green, of a species pure, sound, and exempt from decay. Nothing appeared to receive or to need the attention of an earthly gardener. I thought: how is it that all is so beautiful, since as yet there are no human beings! Ah! Sin has not yet entered. There has been no destruction, no rending asunder. All is sound, all is holy. As yet there has been no healing, no repairing. All is pure, nothing has needed purification.

The plain that I beheld was gently undulating and covered with vegetation. In its center rose a fountain, from all sides of which flowed streams, crossing one another and mingling their waters. I saw in them first a slight movement as of life, and then I saw living things. After that I saw, here and there among the shrubs and bushes, animals peeping forth, as if just roused from sleep. They were very different from those of a later day, not at all timorous. Compared with those of our own time, they were almost as far their superior as men are superior to beasts. They were pure and noble, nimble, and joyous. Words cannot describe them. I was not familiar with many of them, for I saw very few like those we have now. I saw the elephant, the stag, the camel, and even the unicorn. This last I saw also in the ark. It is remarkably gentle and affectionate, not so tall as a horse, its head more rounded in shape [see further below]. I saw no asses, no insects, no wretched, loathsome creatures. These last I have always looked upon as a punishment of sin. But I saw myriads of birds and heard the sweetest notes as in the early morning. There were no birds of prey that I could see, nor did I hear any animals bellowing.

Paradise is still in existence, but it is utterly impossible for humankind to reach it. I have seen that it still exists in all its splendor. It is high above the earth and in an oblique direction from it, like the dark globe of the angels fallen from heaven.

A Further Glance at Paradise

ON *February 13, 1821, as Anne Catherine lay, as usual, absorbed in ecstatic contemplation in the presence of Fr. Limberg and Christian Brentano, the brother of the pilgrim, the latter entered the room with a piece of petrified bone in his hand. It was about the size of an egg and had been found in the River Lippe. He laid it gently on her bed. Still in ecstasy, she took it into her left hand and held it for a few moments; then she opened her eyes and looked steadily at the pilgrim, who fully expected to receive a rebuke for having given her the bone of a brute animal instead of a holy relic. But, still absorbed in contemplation, she exclaimed*:

How did the pilgrim get into that wonderful, that beautiful garden into which I can only look? There he is with that great animal! How can it be! O how beautiful is all I see! I cannot express it, I cannot describe it! O God, how wonderful, how incomprehensible, how powerful, how magnificent, how lovely art Thou in all Thy works! O here is something far above nature! For here there is nothing touched by sin! Here is nothing bad, here all things seem to have just come from the Hand of God!

I see a whole herd of white animals, with hair like masses of curls falling over their backs; they are much taller than men, and yet they run as lightly and nimbly as horses. Their legs are like pillars, and yet so softly they tread! They have a long trunk which they can raise and lower and turn on all sides like an arm, and long snow-white teeth protrude from their mouth. How elegant, how clean they are! These animals are enormous, but so handsome! Their eyes are small, but so intelligent, so bright, so mild— I cannot describe it! They have broad, hanging ears, a tail fine as silk, but so short they cannot reach it with their trunk. O they must be very old, their hair is so long! They have young ones they love tenderly; they play with them like children. They are so intelligent, so gentle, so mild! They go together in such order, as if on some business. Then there are other animals! They are not dogs—they are yellow as gold and have long manes, and faces almost human! O they are lions, but so gentle! They catch one another by the mane and frolic around. And there are sheep and camels, oxen and horses, all white and shining like silk, and wonderfully beautiful white asses! Words cannot say how lovely it all is, or what order and peace and love reign here! They do no harm to one another, they mutually help one another. Most are white, or golden; I see very few dark ones. And what is most astonishing is that all have abodes so well arranged, so beautifully divided off into passages and apartments—and all so neat! One can form no idea of it. I see no human beings; there are none here! Spirits must come and put things in order—we cannot imagine that the animals do it themselves.

Here Anne Catherine paused as if attentively regarding something, and then exclaimed:

There is Frances of Rome![1] And there is Catherine of Ricci![2] High over the beautiful garden floats something like a sun in whose rays the saints are hovering and looking down; there are ever so many of them up above me, and the sun is dazzlingly white. Its rays look like a great white silken carpet on which the saints float, or it is like a great white silk cover shining in the sun's rays. The saints are standing on it and looking down.

O now I know it all! All the water comes from up there, and the lovely garden is the garden of paradise! There are the animals kept, there all is still as God created it, though the garden seems

---

[1] Frances of Rome (1384–March 9, 1440) was an Italian saint who was a wife, mother, mystic, organizer of charitable services, and a Benedictine oblate. She founded a religious community of oblates who share a common life without religious vows. With her husband's consent, Frances practiced continence and advanced in a life of contemplation. Her visions often assumed the form of a drama enacted for her by heavenly personages. She had the gift of miracles and ecstasy as well as the bodily vision of her guardian angel, had revelations concerning purgatory and hell, and foretold the ending of the Western Schism. She could read the secrets of consciences and detect plots of diabolical origin. She was remarkable for her humility and detachment, her obedience and patience.

[2] Catherine de Ricci (April 23, 1522–February 1, 1590) was an Italian Dominican Tertiary nun. She is believed in Catholicism to have had miraculous visions and corporeal encounters with Jesus, both with the infant Jesus and with the adult Jesus, with whom she said she had mystically united in marriage. She is said to have spontaneously bled with the wounds of the crucified Christ. She is venerated for her mystic visions and has been honored as a saint by the Catholic Church.

to me much larger now than paradise was at first. No man can enter therein! The wonderfully clear, the magnificent, holy water that there springs forth and flows in limpid streams through the garden of the animals, forms around the whole of paradise a great liquid wall, not a lake—a wall! and O what a wonderful, sparkling wall it is! The top is formed of clear drops like precious stones, like the morning dew on the hedges—such is this wall at the top, but clear, transparent as crystal.

At the base it flows in tiny rivulets that unite and form further down an immense cataract. O how it roars! No one can hear it without being deafened! All the waters of our earth come from there; but when they reach us they are altogether changed, they are quite impure![1]

---

[1] Elsewhere Anne Catherine says: "I was astonished to see the pilgrim there, sometimes as a tiny figure in the distance, sometimes close at hand. I had the feeling, and then received a teaching, that all waters descended from on high, but became turbid and mixed along the way. So also have human beings descended, becoming ever darker and altered. The holy waters of the promised land, and also of earlier lands, were charged with great powers above, but all these lands are gone, sunken away through the effects of sin. All things, also ourselves, have been flushed out as impure."

The mountain of the prophets [see further below] also receives its water and moisture from paradise, which is situated as far above it as the sky is far above our earth; and the place in which I see the saints is as far above paradise as is paradise above the mountain of the prophets. By the time the great cataract, formed by the waters of paradise, reaches the mountain, it is changed into clouds. No human being can reach that mountain, nothing is seen above it but clouds.

In paradise there are no buildings of stone, but only green groves and alleys and walks for the animals. The trees are enormously high, their trunks so straight and elegant! I see white, yellow, red, brown, and black—no, not black, but shining steel-blue. And what wonderful flowers! I see quantities of roses, chiefly white, very large, growing on high bushes, some of them running up into the trees; and there are also red ones and tall white lilies. The grass looks soft as silk. But I can only see it—I cannot feel it, for it is too far away. O what beautiful apples! so large and yellow! And how long the leaves of the trees are! The fruits in the garden of the nuptial house look perfectly deformed in comparison with these; and yet they are unspeakably beautiful when compared with those of earth.

I see numbers of birds, but no words could tell their beauty, their brilliancy of color, their variety! They build their nests in flowers, in clusters of the loveliest flowers. I see doves flying over the wall with tiny leaves and branches in their beak. I think the leaves and flowers I sometimes received for relief in my pains must have come from this garden.

I see no serpents like those that crawl the earth, but there is a beautiful little yellow animal with a serpent's head. It is large around the body and tapering off toward the tail; it has four legs, and when it sits up on its hind feet, it is as tall as a child. Its forefeet are short, its eyes bright and intelligent, and it is uncommonly swift and graceful. I only see a few of them. It was an animal like this that seduced Eve.

How wonderful! There is a gateway in the water wall and there lie two men! They are asleep, their back resting on the glittering water wall, their hands joined on their breast, their feet turned, one toward the other. They have long fair curls. They are spirits clothed in long white mantles, and they have under their arms small rolls of shining writings; their crooks lie near them. They are prophets! Yes, I feel it! They are in communication with the man on the mountain of the prophets. And on what wondrous couches they repose! Flowers grow around them in brilliant, regular forms, and surround their head, white, yellow, red, green, blue, shining like the rainbow.[1]

On the following day, the pilgrim found Anne Catherine a little troubled at her confessor's having laughed at her vision of the preceding evening, as at things unreasonable and impossible. He chided her for her uneasiness, asking how she could complain of her enemies' looking upon her as an impostor, since she herself was so ready to treat as extravagant the wonders shown her by God. At this she repeated the above recital, adding thereto the following details:

I stood high up, outside the walls of paradise, over which and through which I could see. In several parts of it I caught a glimpse of myself reflected, and I looked incredibly large. Paradise is surrounded by drops of water—round, three-cornered, and of various pure, regular shapes—which touch one another without mingling and form all kinds of figures and flowers, like pictures woven in linen.[2] One could see through it, though not so distinctly as over it. The extreme top was colored like the rainbow, but it had no figures; it arose toward the heavens as does the rainbow that we see on earth. Toward the lower part of this Wall are seen crystals melting into tiny streams like silver threads that unite to form the huge cataract. So great was its roar that I think to hear it would be to die. It still sounds in my ears! At a vast distance below it vaporizes and forms clouds from which the

---

[1] Elsewhere Anne Catherine says: "I always see the place where Adam was created from the earth as a beautiful white mountain rising before the entrance to paradise, where Enoch and Elijah now lie." And again: "Enoch was taken up to paradise. There he waits at the entrance gate, whence with another [Elijah] he will come again before the Last Day."

[2] Calderon in his drama *La Vie est un Songe*, makes the Eternal Wisdom address the waters in these words: "Divide, ye waters, divide! Rise up to heaven and form the crystal firmament, that the lyre, which there sits on a throne of light, may temper its beat in thy limpid waves!" CB

mountain of the prophets receives all its waters. The top of the gateway was arched and colored, but down toward the middle of the wall the light was not so clear. It was as when we see one thing through another.

The sides of the wall against which the prophets leaned were neither drops nor crystal, but one solid surface, snow-white like milk, like the finest silk. The prophets had long, yellowish white hair. Their eyes were closed, and they lay as if on flower beds; their hands were crossed on their breast, and they were wrapped in long, bright mantles. Their faces were turned earthward, and encircling their brows was a halo of many colors, like the glory of the saints, the extremities paling off into light. Their rolls of writings had no knobs; they were thin and brilliant, with blue and gold lettering. Their crooks were white and slender, and variegated flowers seemed to be growing around them. The gate opened toward the east.

Some of the elephants had smooth skins, not thick curls like the others, and the little ones ran like lambs between their feet.[1] They paired off with their young into great groves. I saw also white-haired camels, very beautiful, bluish asses striped, and animals like large white cats, spotted yellow and blue. The yellow serpent seemed to serve the other animals. In the limpid streams I saw shining fish and other animals; but I saw no vermin, no disgusting things. All the animals had separate abodes that were approached by different roads.

Paradise is as large as our earth. It has round, smooth hills planted with beautiful trees; the highest I thought the one on which Adam rested. Toward the north was an egress, but not through a gate; it was like a gleam of twilight, like an aperture, like a steep descent, and it seemed to me that the waters of the deluge had been there poured forth. Near the great waters from which the cataract fell I saw somewhat lower and to the side a

---

[1] On November 1, 1823, Anne Catherine said: "Of the mammoths—those immense animals so numerous before the deluge—a very young pair entered the ark last and remained near the entrance. In the times of Nimrod, Jamshid, and Semiramis, I still saw many. But they were constantly being hunted and soon became extinct."

broad green field scattered over with enormous bones bleached white, which seemed to have been cast up by the waters.[1] Highest of all is the crystal wall; a little lower down run the silvery threads; and then appears the vast body of waters, in which I saw large fishes, whence dashes the cataract with its deafening roar. This last is lost in the clouds that supply the mountain of the prophets with its waters. The mountain is much lower than paradise and lies toward the east; even there everything is more like our earth.[2]

Unicorns

UNICORNS still exist and herd together. I know of a piece of the horn of one of these animals that is for sick beasts what blessed objects are for men. I have often seen that unicorns still exist, but far remote from the abodes of men, away up in the valleys around the mountain of the prophets. In size they are something like a colt with slender legs; they can climb steep heights and stand on a very narrow ledge, their feet drawn close together. They cast off their hoofs like shells or shoes, for I have often seen them scattered around. They have long yellowish hair, very thick and long around the neck and breast; it looks like wreaths. They live to a great age. On their forehead is a single horn, an ell in length, which curls up toward the back of the head, and which they shed at certain periods. It is sought after and preserved as something very precious.

The unicorns are very timid, so shy that one cannot approach them, and they live at peace among themselves and with other animals. The males and females dwell apart and come together only at certain times, for they are chaste and produce not many young. It is very difficult to see or catch them, as they live far back

---

[1] "Among these were breastbones, pelvic bones, and enormous teeth, shining like an ivory crucifix. I knew not whence they might have come."

[2] Anne Catherine adds: "I saw works of men, structures, etc. I saw it all again last night. I saw the prophets moving about among huts as though they were engaged upon some business. I saw again the chariot [see below, 'The Mountain of the Prophets']. It was as though I saw all the same things, but they were now fresher, quicker with life, more fully in bloom."

behind the other animals, over which they exercise a wonderful empire. Even the most venomous, the most horrible, seem to regard them with a species of respect. Serpents and other frightful things coil themselves up and lie humbly on their backs when a unicorn approaches and breathes on them. They have a kind of alliance with the most savage beasts: they mutually protect one another. When danger threatens a unicorn, the others spread terror on all sides while the unicorn hides behind them, but in its turn it protects them from their enemies, for all withdraw in affright from the secret and marvelous power of the unicorn's breath. It must be the purest of the lower animals, since all have so great reverence for it. Wherever it feeds, wherever it drinks, all venomous things withdraw.

It seems to me that the unicorn is looked upon as something holy, since it is said that it rests its head only upon the bosom of a pure virgin. This signifies that flesh issued pure and holy only from the bosom of the blessed Virgin Mary; that degenerate flesh was regenerated in her; or that in her for the first time flesh became pure. In her the ungovernable was vanquished; in her what was savage was subdued; in her unrestrained humanity became pure and tractable; in her bosom was the poison withdrawn from the earth.

I saw these animals also in paradise, but much more beautiful. Once I saw them harnessed to the chariot of Elijah when he appeared to a man of the Old Testament. I have seen them on wild, raging torrents, and running swiftly in deep, narrow, rugged valleys; and I have also seen far distant places where lie heaps of their bones on shores and in underground caves."

The Mountain of the Prophets

ONE day about noon the sun was shining through the little window of my room, when I saw a holy man with two female religious approach my bed. They were dazzling with light. They presented me a large book like a missal and said: "If you can study this book, you will see what belongs to a religious." I replied: "I shall read it right away," and I took the book on my knee. It was Latin, but I understood every word, and I read it eagerly. They left it with me and disappeared. The leaves were of parchment, written in red and gold letters. There were some pictures of the early saints in it. It was bound in yellow and had no clasps. I took it with me to the convent and read it attentively. When I had read a little, it was always taken away from me.

One day it was lying on the table when several of the sisters came in and tried to take it off with them, but they could not move it from its place. More than once it was said to me: "You have still so many leaves to read." Years after, when I was rapt in spirit to the mountain of the prophets, I saw this same book among many other prophetic writings of all times and places. It was shown me as the share I was to have in these treasures. Other things that I had received on various occasions, and that I had kept for a long time, were also preserved here. At present I have still five leaves to read; but I must have leisure for it, that I may leave its contents after me.[1]

This mysterious book was not merely symbolical, it was a real book, a volume of prophecies. It formed a part, as will be seen further on, of the treasure of sacred writings preserved upon what Anne Catherine called the "mountain of the prophets." These writings are transmitted miraculously to those who, by the infusion of prophetic light, have been rendered capable of reading them. The book in question treated of the essence and signification of the religious state, its rank in the Church, and its mission in every age. It also taught those to whom such a vocation was given what service they could render to the Church in their own time.

What Anne Catherine read in this book was afterward unfolded to her in a series of pictures. When she recited a psalm, the Magnificat, *the* Benedictus, *the* Gospel of St. John, *a prayer from the* Liturgy, *or the* Litany of the Blessed Virgin, *the words unfolded, as it were, like the ovary that contains the seed, and their history and meaning were presented to her contemplation. It was the same with this book. In it she learned that the chief end of the religious life is union with the heavenly*

---

[1] Brentano recorded this in his notes on December 20, 1819, and Anne Catherine died in 1824—that is, five years later.

Bridegroom, and in this general view she distinctly perceived her own duty, with the means, obstacles, labors, pains, and mortifications that would further its accomplishment. All this she saw not only in what referred to her own sanctification, but also in what related to the situation and wants of the whole Church. She had not received the grace of religious vocation for herself alone. She was to be, as it were, a treasury for this grace, with all the favors attached thereto, that she might preserve it to the Church at a time in which the Lord's vineyard was being laid waste. Therefore, all she learned in the prophetic book, and all she did in accordance with its teachings, bore the stamp of expiation and satisfaction for the failings of others. Her spiritual labors were performed less for herself than for her neighbor; they were a harvest, a conquest, whose fruits and spoils were for the good of the whole Church.

The more closely Anne Catherine studied this mysterious book, the more extended became her visions, the more did they influence her whole inner and outer life. She saw the harmony of the pictures presented to her soul, whether with one another, or with her own mission; she saw that they embraced in their entirety the history of a soul seeking her celestial Spouse. She sighs after him, she tends toward him, she prepares all that is needful for her espousals; but she is continually delayed and perplexed by the loss or destruction of many necessary articles, and by the malicious efforts of others to thwart and annoy her. From time to time impending events were shown her in symbolical pictures, which never failed to be realized. She was warned of the hindrances caused by her own faults and by her too great condescension to others; but this foreknowledge never removed difficulties from her path. It did indeed strengthen and enlighten her, but the victory was still to be won by many a hard struggle.

In the second week of Advent, Anne Catherine was taken by her angel guide to the highest peak of a mountain in Tibet, quite inaccessible to man. Here she saw Elijah guarding the treasures of knowledge communicated to humankind by the angels and prophets since the Creation. She was told that the mysterious prophetic book in which she had been allowed to read belonged here. This was not her first visit. She had often been brought hither by her angel, and also to the terrestrial paradise not far distant. These places seemed to be closely connected, as in both she met the same holy custodians. Her own prophetic light gave her a certain right to participate in the riches preserved in them, and she had

*need of the supernatural gifts there bestowed upon her for the continu-
ance of her expiatory task. She could retain only a general impression of
what she saw, which she reproduced in very imperfect sketches.*

*The following extended note by Brentano, added later, may serve as
an introduction to what follows:*

"Mountain of the prophets" is the name given by Anne
Catherine to a place high above all the mountains of the
world, to which she was taken for the first time on
December 10, 1819 in her ecstatic state of dream-journey-
ing, and again several times later. There she saw the books
of prophetic revelation of all ages and all peoples preserved
in a tent and examined and superintended by someone
who reminded her partly of John the Evangelist and partly
of Elijah—particularly of the latter, since she perceived
the chariot which had transported that prophet from
the earth standing here on the heights near the tent and
overgrown with green plants. This person then told her
that he compared with a great book lying before him all
the books of prophetic knowledge that had ever been
given (often in a very confused state) or would in future be
given to humankind; and that much of these he crossed
out or destroyed in the fire burning at his side. Humankind, he said, was not yet capable of receiving these gifts,
another must first come, and so forth.

Anne Catherine saw all this on a green island in a lake of
clear water. On the island were many towers of different
shapes, surrounded by gardens. She had the impression
that these towers were treasuries and reservoirs of the wisdom of different peoples, and that under the island—
which was full of murmuring streams—lay the source of
rivers held to be sacred (the Ganges among them), whose
waters issued forth at the foot of the mountain range. The
direction in which she was led to this mountain of the
prophets was always (taking into account the starting-
point of her journey) toward the highest part of Central
Asia. She described places, natural scenery, human beings,
animals, and plants of the region she traversed before

being carried up through a lonely and desolate space—as if through clouds—to the place mentioned above. On her return journey she was carried down through the region of clouds once more, and then again traversed lands rich in luxuriant vegetation and full of animals and birds, until she reached the Ganges and saw the religious ceremonies of the Hindus beside this river. Anne Catherine once said that the source of the Ganges was an unknown lake, and that from just such a place as this had Zarathustra received his book.

The geographical situation of this place, and Anne Catherine's statement that she had seen everything up there overgrown with living green, reminded someone who read her account twenty years later of traditions about a place of this kind (sometimes with a similar inhabitant) in the religions of several Asiatic peoples. The prophet Elijah is known to the Muslims (under the name of Al-Khidr, "the Green One") as a wonderful half-angelic being who dwells in the north on a mountain known as Qaf, celebrated in many religious and poetical writings, and there watches over secrets at the source of the River of Life. The Hindus called their holy mountain Meru, while to the Chinese it was Kunlun—both connected with representations of a state of paradise, and both situated on the heights of Central Asia, where Anne Catherine saw the mountain of the prophets. The ancient Persians also believed in such a place and called it Alborz or Elburz. According to Isa. 14:13 ("I will sit in the mountain of the covenant, in the sides of the north"), the Babylonians would seem to have held a similar belief. That they, like the Persians and Muslims, placed this mountain in the north is explained by their geographical position as regards the mountains of Central Asia.

LAST night I journeyed over different parts of the promised land. I saw it just as it was in our Master's time. I went first to Bethlehem, as if to announce the coming of the holy family, and then I

17

followed a route already well known to me and saw pictures of the public life of Jesus. I saw him distributing the bread by the hands of two of his disciples, and then explaining a parable. The people sat on the slope of a hill under tall trees that bore all their leaves on top like a crown. Underneath were bushes with red and yellow berries, like brambleberries. A stream of water ran down the hill and branched off into other small streams. I gathered some of the grass: it was soft, fine as silk, like thick moss. But when I tried to touch other objects, I could not. I found they were only pictures of times long past, though the grass I really felt. The Master was, as usual, in a long, yellowish woolen tunic. His hair, parted in the middle, fell low upon his shoulders. His face was peaceful, earnest, and beaming with light, his forehead very white and shining. The two who distributed the bread broke it into pieces which the men, women, and children ran to receive; they ate and then sat down. Behind the Master was a brook.

I saw many other pictures as I passed rapidly from place to place. Leaving Jerusalem, I went toward the east and met several great bodies of water and mountains that the three kings had crossed on their journey to Bethlehem. Here was much white sand punctuated with fragments of black rock. I came also to countries in which many people lived, but I did not enter them. I traveled mostly over deserts.

At last I reached a very cold region, and I was led up higher and higher. Along the mountain chain from west to east was a great road over which troops of men were traveling. They were diminutive, but very active, and they carried little standards. I saw some of another race, very tall. They were not Christians. Their road led down the mountain. But mine led up to a region of incredible beauty, where the air was balmy and the vegetation green and luxuriant—flowers of marvelous loveliness, charming groves, dense woods. Numbers of animals sported around, apparently harmless.

No human beings inhabited this region, no human being had ever been there, and from the great road only clouds could be seen. I saw herds of nimble animals with very slender legs like young roebucks; they had no horns, their skin was clear brown with black spots. I saw a short black animal something like the hog, and others like great goats, but still more like the roebucks; they were tame, bright-eyed, and quick on their feet. I saw others like fat sheep with wigs of wool and thick tails; others like asses, but spotted; flocks of little yellow nanny-goats, and herds of little horses; great long-legged birds running swiftly and numbers of lovely tiny ones of all colors, sporting in perfect freedom, as if ignorant of humankind's existence.

From this paradisal region I mounted still higher, as if through the clouds, and at last came to the summit of the mountain, where I saw wonders! It was a vast plain surrounding a lake in which was a green island connected with the shore by a strip of verdant land. The island was surrounded by great trees like cedars. I was taken up to the top of one of them, whence, holding firmly to the branches, I saw the whole island at once. There were several slender towers with a little portico on each, as if a chapel were built over the gate. These porticoes were all covered with fresh verdure—moss or ivy—for the vegetation here was luxuriant. The towers were about as high as bell-towers, but very slender, reminding me of the tall columns in the old cities I had seen on my journey. They were of different forms, cylindrical and octagonal; the former built of huge stones, polished and veined with moon-shaped roofs; the latter, which had broad, projecting roofs, were covered with raised figures and ornaments by means of which one might climb to the top. The stones were colored brown, red, black, and arranged in various patterns. The towers were not higher than the trees, on one of which I stood, though they seemed to be equal to them in number.

The trees were a kind of fir with needle-shaped leaves. They bore yellow fruit covered with scales, not so long as pineapples, more like common apples. They had numerous trunks covered, toward the root, with gnarled bark—but higher up it was smoother; they were straight, symmetrical, and stood far enough apart not to touch. The whole island was covered with verdure, thick, fine, and short—not grass, but a plant with fine curled leaves like moss, as soft and nice as the softest cushion. There was no trace of a road or path. Near each tower was a small garden laid off in beds, with a great variety of shrubs and beautiful blooming trees—all was green, the gardens differing from one another as much as the towers. As from my tree I glanced over the island, I could see the lake at one end, but not the mountain. The water was wonderfully clear and sparkling. It flowed across the island in streams that were lost underground.

Opposite the narrow slip of land in the green plain was a long tent of gray stuff inside of which, at the further end, hung broad colored stripes, painted or embroidered in all kinds of figures. A table stood in the center. Around it were stone seats without backs; they looked like cushions, and they too were covered with living verdure. In the middle and most honorable seat, behind the low, oval, stone table, was a manly, holy, shining figure sitting cross-legged in Eastern fashion, and writing with a reed on a large roll of parchment.[1] The pen looked like a little branch. Right and left lay great books and parchment rolls on rods with knobs at either end. By the tent was a furnace in the earth, like a deep hole, in which burned a fire whose flames rose not above its mouth.

The whole country was like a beautiful green island up in the clouds. The sky above was indescribably clear, though I saw only a semicircle of bright rays, much larger however than we ever see. The scene was inexpressibly holy, solitary, charming! While I gazed upon it, it seemed as if I understood all that it signified. But I knew that I should not be able to remember it. My guide was visible until we reached the tent, and then he disappeared.

As I gazed in wonder, I thought, "Why am I here? And why must I, poor creature, see all this?" And the figure from the tent spoke: "It is because you have a share in it!" This only surprised me more, and I descended—or rather, I floated down—to where he sat in the tent. He was clothed like the spirits I am accustomed

---

[1] Elsewhere Anne Catherine says this man seemed to her to be the apostle John.

to see, his look and bearing like John the Baptist[1] or Elijah. The books and rolls were very old and precious. On some of them were metallic figures or ornaments in relief; for instance, a man with a book in his hand. The figure told me—or informed me in some way—that these books contained all the holiest things that had ever come from humankind. He examined and compared all, and threw what was false into the fire near the tent. He told me that he was there to guard everything until the time would come to make use of it, which time might have already come, had there not been so many obstacles. I asked if he did not feel tired waiting so long, and he replied "In God there is no time!" He said that I must see everything, and he took me out and showed me around. He said also that humankind did not yet deserve what was kept there.

The tent was about as high as two men, as long as from here to the church in the city, and about half as broad. The top was gathered into a knot and fastened to a string that went up and was lost in the air. I wondered what supported it. At the four corners were columns that one could almost span with both hands; they were veined like the polished towers and capped by green knobs. The tent was open in front and on the sides.

In the middle of the table lay an immense book that could be opened and shut. It seemed to be fastened to the table, and it was to this the man referred to see if the others were right. I felt there was a door under the table and that a sacred treasure was kept there. The moss-covered seats were placed far enough from the table to allow one to walk around between them and it; behind them lay numbers of books, right and left, the latter destined for the flames. He led me all around them, and I noticed on the covers pictures of men carrying ladders, books, churches, towers, tablets, etc. He told me again that he examined them and burned what was false and useless. Humankind, he said, was not yet prepared for their contents—another must come first.

He took me around the shore of the lake. Its surface was on a level with the island. The waters at my feet ran under the moun-

---

[1] In a footnote related to this present article Brentano speaks instead of the apostle John [the Evangelist] and Elijah.

tain by numerous channels and reappeared below in springs. It seemed as if all this quarter of the world received thereby health and benediction; it never overflowed above. The descent of the mountain on the east and south was green and covered with beautiful flowers; on the west and north there was verdure, but no flowers. At the extremity of the lake I crossed over without a bridge and went all around among the towers. The ground was like a bed of thick, firm moss, as if hollow underneath. The towers arose out of it, and the gardens around them were watered by rivulets that flowed either to or from the lake, I know not which. There were no walks in the gardens, though they were all laid out in order. I saw roses far larger than ours—red, white, yellow, and dark—and a species of lily, very tall flowers, blue with white streaks, and also a stalk as high as a tree with large palm leaves. It bore on the top a flower like a large plate.

I understood that in the towers were preserved the greatest treasures of Creation, and I felt that holy bodies rested in them. Between two of them I saw standing a singular chariot with four low wheels. It had two seats and a small one in front. Four persons could easily be accommodated, and—like everything else on the island—it was all covered with vegetation or green mold. It had no pole. It was ornamented with carved figures so well executed that at first sight I thought them alive. The box was formed of thin metallic open-worked figures; the wheels were heavier than those of Roman chariots, yet it all seemed light enough to be drawn by men. I looked at everything closely, because the man said "You have a share herein, and you can now take possession of it." I could not understand what share I had in it. "What have I to do," I thought, "with this singular looking chariot, these towers, these books!"

I had a deep feeling of the sanctity of the place. I felt that with its waters the salvation of many generations had flowed down into the valleys, that humankind itself had come from this mountain, and had sunk ever lower, and lower; and I also felt that heaven's gifts for men were here stored, guarded, purified, and prepared. I had a clear perception of it all; but I could not retain it, and now have only a general impression.

When I re-entered the tent, the man again addressed me in the same words: "You have a part in all this, you can even take possession of it!" And, as I represented to him my incapacity, he said with calm assurance: "You will soon return to me!" He went not out of the tent while I was there, but moved around the table and the books. The former was not so green as the seats, nor the seats as the things near the towers, for it was not so damp here. The ground in the tent and everything it contained were moss-grown—table, seats, and all. The foot of the table seemed to serve as a chest to hold something sacred. I had an impression that a holy body reposed therein. I thought there was under it a subterranean vault and that a sweet odor was exhaled from it. I felt that the man was not always in the tent. He received me as if he knew me and had waited for my coming. He told me confidently that I should return, and then showed me the way down.

I went toward the south, by the steep mountain, through the clouds, and into the delightful region where there were so many animals. There was not a single one up above. I saw numerous springs gushing from the mountain, playing in cascades, and running down in streams. I saw birds larger than geese, in color like a partridge, with three claws in front of the foot and one behind, a tail somewhat flat, and a long neck. There were other birds with bluish plumage very like the ostrich, but rather smaller. I saw all the other animals.

In this journey I saw many more human beings than in the others. Once I crossed a small river that I felt flowed from the lake above. I followed it awhile and then lost sight of it. I came to a place where poor people of various races lived in huts. I think they were Christian captives. I saw brown-complexioned men with white kerchiefs on their head bringing food to them in wicker baskets; they reached it to them the whole length of their arm and then fled away in fright as if exposed to danger. They lived in rude huts in a ruined city. I saw water in which great, strong reeds grew, and I came again to the river, which is very broad here, and full of rocks, sandbanks, and beautiful green weeds, among which it danced. It was the same river that flowed from the mountain, and that—as a little stream—I had crossed higher up. A great many dark-complexioned people—men, women, and children in various costumes—were on the rocks and islets, drinking and bathing. They seemed to have come from a distance. It reminded me of what I had seen at the Jordan in the Holy Land. A very tall man stood among them, seemingly their priest. He filled their vessels with water. I saw many other things. I was not far from the country where Francis Xavier used to be. I crossed the sea over innumerable islands.

I know why I went to the mountain. My book lies among the writings on the table and I shall get it again to read the last five leaves. The man who sits at the table will come again in due time. His chariot remains there as a perpetual memorial. He mounted up there in it, and men—to their astonishment—will behold him coming again in the same. Here upon this mountain—the highest in the world, whose summit no one has ever reached—were the sacred treasures and secrets concealed when sin spread among men. The water, the island, the towers—all are to guard these treasures. By the water up there are all things refreshed and renewed. The river flowing from it, whose waters the people venerate, has power to strengthen; therefore is it esteemed more highly than wine. All men, all good things, have come down from above, and all that is to be secured from destruction is there preserved.

The man on the mountain knew me, for I have a share in it. We know each other, we belong together. I cannot express it well, but we are like a seed going through the whole world. Paradise is not far from the mountain. Once before I saw that Elijah lived in a garden near paradise.

I have again seen the prophet mountain. The man in the tent reached to a figure floating over him from heaven leaves and books, and received others in return. He who floated above reminded me very much of John. He was more agile, pleasing, and lighter than the man in the tent, who had something sterner, more energetic and unbending about him; the former was to the latter as the New to the Old Testament, so I may call one John, the other Elijah. It seemed as if Elijah presented to John revelations that had been fulfilled, and received new ones from him.

Then I suddenly saw from the white sea a jet of water shoot up like a crystal ray. It branched into innumerable jets and drops like immense cascades, and fell down upon different parts of the earth, and I saw men in houses, in huts, in cities all over the world, enlightened by it, and as though inebriated with the knowing, expressing, and proclaiming of divine things. It began at once to produce fruit in them.[1]

Last night I made a long journey, chiefly to the mountain of the prophets, and paradise in its vicinity. All was as usual on the mountain, the man under the tent writing and arranging books and rolls of parchment, erasing many things, and burning others. I saw him giving leaves [of books] to doves, which flew away with them. I had also a vision of the Holy Spirit—a winged figure in a triangle surrounded by bands of light of seven different colors, which spread over the spiritual church floating below and over all in communication with her. In this vision I felt that the effusion of the Holy Spirit exercises an influence over all nature. I stood above the earth near the mountain of the prophets and saw the waters that fall from it spread out like a transparent, many-colored veil above the earth, and I saw all sorts of things shining through it. One color sprang from another and produced a different effect. When the veil is rent, the rain descends.[2]

The mountain of the prophets receives its water and moisture from paradise, which is situated as far above it as the sky is far above our earth; and the place in which I see the saints is as far above paradise as paradise is above the mountain of the prophets.

---

[1] On the day following this vision, on the feast of St. John the Evangelist, Anne Catherine beheld St. Peter's Basilica shining like the sun, its rays streaming over all the world. "I was told," she said, "that this referred to St. John's *Apocalypse*. Various individuals would be enlightened by it and they would impart their knowledge to the whole world. I had a very distinct vision, but I cannot relate it." During the octave she had constant visions of the Church, of which, however, she could relate but little. Nor could she give a clear idea of the connection existing between them and the prophet mountain, but we may infer from the pilgrim's notes that they formed a cycle of visions singularly grand. See "Apocalypse" in *Inner Life and Worlds of Soul & Spirit*, for what Anne Catherine was able to recall from these visions.

[2] At this juncture, we find the following two paragraphs: "These effusions take place at certain seasons commemorative of the saints and their victories. The feast of a saint is his true harvest day. On it he dispenses his gifts as a tree does its fruits. What souls do not receive in this outpouring of spiritual gifts falls upon the earth as rain and dew; in this way does a superabundance of rain

By the time the great cataract, formed by the waters of paradise, reaches the mountain, it is changed into clouds. No human being can reach that mountain, nothing is seen above it but clouds."[1]

Again I saw the man on the mountain busy at his writing under the tent, as usual. It always seems to me that he is John; but I know also that John is long dead, and buried on Patmos, so that none of his bones can be here. It seems to me also that the body of the spirit writing here lies in a vault beneath the table, from which he sometimes emerges and into which he then descends again.

When Jesus said to Peter, "If I will that he tarry till I come, what is that to you?" (John 21:22), I saw a picture of John's death in Ephesus: how he lay himself down in his own grave to die, and from there spoke with his disciples, as I have described before. I saw also that his body is not upon this earth.

---

become a chastisement from God. I often see wicked people in fertile places nourished by the fruits of the earth, and good men in sterile regions receiving into their own souls the gifts of the Holy Spirit. Were humankind and the earth in perfect harmony, there would be paradise here below. Prayer governs the weather, and the days marked in the old weather tables are the days on which such distributions are made. When it says: 'If it rain on the third day of Pentecost, the harvest will not be gathered dry,' this may mean: if the spiritual gifts poured out on humankind at Pentecost are received by them only in small measure, they will be changed into rain, which will fall upon them as a chastisement. I see the life of nature intimately connected with that of the soul.

"Wind also is something wonderful. I often see a storm bearing sickness from a far-off land; it looks like a globe full of evil spirits. Violent winds affect me painfully. I have always had a horror of them. And from my very childhood, shooting stars have been hateful to me; for wherever they fall, the air is full of bad spirits. When as a child I watched the rising and setting of the sun, I used to hail it as a creature endued with life. I thought: He weeps over the numerous sins he is forced to witness! Moonlight would be agreeable to me on account of the peaceful silence, were it not that I know the sins it covers and its powerful influence over man's sensual nature; for the moon is more deeply enervating than the sun."

[1] As Anne Catherine lay in vision, quite insensate in a darkened room, the pilgrim held out before her a page from these present writings, whereupon she suddenly pronounced: "These pages are written in a shining script; they were written by the man whom I saw sitting at his writing yesterday night [that is, Brentano himself]. He must have previously been at the side of that other person—the one with the broken heart—of whom I have recently understood she

I saw between the east and north a shining realm, like a sun, and John therein, mediating something—as though receiving something from above, then passing it on. This realm seemed still to belong to the earth, and yet was far away and inaccessible. I saw also that it is in this region that paradise—though now separated off—still hovers. Four such regions I saw, one at each end of the earth, but I cannot recall what they contained. On this occasion I did not see the realm of John as that of the mountain of the prophets (for I was not then present there), but rather as a luminous body.

When I behold the world as a globe, and stand directly above Jerusalem, its round disc lies at an angle to me; and it is not entirely round, but flattened somewhat at either end. When I take up a position opposite Jerusalem, the mountain of the prophets—the place where John is, and to which also paradise belongs—comes into view situated between the north and the east, still within the space of the globe itself. I can tell it belongs with the earth because if I move to a position further south above the globe, I see the region lying at the outermost edge rise up with respect to the heaven beyond, and then a ring of light surrounding this lofty, apparent[1] mountain. Whether this region is

---

will say many things to him [she was referring to herself]. His words are written with milk, white and luminous. The writings on the mountain [of the prophets] are written with water. The two shall flow together, and how thriving that will be! O, if only you could see how the rays from the lake of the prophet illuminate all, how they run all together—I cannot express it!"

Through these words of Anne Catherine, the pilgrim understood incontrovertibly that, just as she perceived relics and other sacred things shining (as also her own hair and stigmata, and the crusts that sometimes formed upon the latter), so shone for her also written words that really—and not as some allegory only—portrayed the truth of her inner experiences. It was as though light had flowed from the pen that scribed them, so that to her the pages were luminous also. And so did she say that he who wrote these pages did so not of himself only, but with grace from God, that no other man than he could do this—for it was as though he saw all himself.

[1] In the overall context, the German word used here, "scheinbar," might also be rendered as "lustrous," or even better, "etheric," in the sense of its earlier connotation of the spiritual medium of light.

in fact separate from the earth, or in some way forms a part of it, I cannot say, because the ring [of light] obscures my view. But it seems to me the two belong together.

Paradise lies in this region also, but more to the east; and from its high station I see all the water running down, etc. I see upon the earth four such places that are encircled with light, but of the other three I know nothing but that they are darker and distinguished by mist, or sometimes a reddish glow. The three form together with the first a square, as if the four interpenetrate the sphere like a cross. But I know nothing more about those three. The mountain of the prophets is, however, all light.

I see the globe at its rim—where it touches the space—surrounded or framed with many different colors, lustres, and clouds. It is quite pure and clearly-defined, not at all uneven, excepting some few places. Behind the mountain of the prophets is a wide field littered with whitened bones.

Again I found myself on the mountain of the prophets, where I beheld the apparition that seemed no other than John; and also another person whom I saw coming and going, though whither or whence I could not tell. An uncommonly large number of scrolls lay there in a heap, and a fire burned close by. The spirit there had with him a large book composed of many rolls to which he transferred extracts from piled-up scrolls. I received also a teaching regarding the pile of writings, but can unfortunately no longer recall what I was told, except that it had to do with the setting apart of something good, the redemption of debts, and what must be consigned to the flames. The great book, I learned, must one day be fully scribed; and when I learned this, I thought to myself that such a task will require a very long time indeed.

I saw the whole mountain—the towers, Elijah's chariot, the waters—all just as I had seen it before, though on this occasion everything was lovelier, purer, more living. The whole region seemed improved, those dwelling there not so dark, and the region above which the mountain rose not so desolate. It was as though summer had overlaid winter.

Noah's Sacrifice

From Adam, Eve, & Other
Old Testament Figures to Job

Adam and Eve

I SAW Adam created, not in paradise, but in the region in which Jerusalem was subsequently situated.[1] This region lay before the entrance to paradise, where I now sometimes see Enoch and Elias resting, as though asleep. I saw him come forth glittering and white from a mound of yellow earth, as if out of a mold. The sun was shining and I thought (I was only a child when I saw it) that the sunbeams drew Adam out of the hillock. He was, as it were, born of the earth. God blessed the earth, which was a virgin, and she became his mother. He did not instantly step forth from the earth. Some time elapsed before his appearance.

He lay in the hillock on his left side, his arm thrown over his head, a light vapor covering him as with a veil. I saw a figure in his right side, and I became conscious that it was Eve, and that she would be drawn from him in paradise by God. God called him. The hillock opened, and Adam stepped gently forth. There were no trees around, only little flowers. I had seen the animals also, coming forth from the earth in pure singleness, the females separate from the males.[2]

Adam was not such as we are, but a man created after the like-

---

[1] Anne Catherine says elsewhere that she saw Adam and Eve in paradise one day only.

[2] On another occasion Anne Catherine says: "I saw Adam in the mountain before the entrance to paradise in a space like a mussel-shell [most likely in the following, oft-repeated, form shown below], his arm thrown over his head. He was covered as with a light mist, as though arising from an inflorescence, and stepped forth upon God's call. The earth was a beautiful yellow. He was not a human being like us, for in him the two sexes had not separated, nor were they

ness of God. He was one; but the foundation, the essence, of woman, of Eve—whom God thereafter fashioned from his rib—was also in him. This I knew because within him I beheld a form that represented conceiving, protecting, nourishing—the chalice-form of motherhood:

And now I saw Adam borne up on high to a garden, to paradise. God led all the animals before him in paradise, and he named them. They followed him and gamboled around him, for all things served him before he sinned. All that he named, afterward followed him to earth. Eve had not yet been formed from him.

Night and day are often spoken of, but at that time I beheld no night, only perhaps that the sun did not yet shine.

I saw Adam in paradise among the plants and flowers, and not far from the fountain that played in its center. He was awaking, as if from sleep. Although his person was more like to flesh than to spirit, yet he was dazzlingly white. He wondered at nothing, nor was he astonished at his own existence. He went around among the trees and the animals as if he were used to them all, like a man inspecting his fields.

Near the tree by the water arose a hill. On it I saw Adam reclining on his left side, his left hand under his cheek. God sent a deep sleep upon him and he was rapt in vision. Then from his right side—from the same place in which the side of Jesus was opened

---

side-by-side, for in him were the male and the female as yet a oneness. Also, and previously, I saw how the animals arose also in a pure unity from the earth, and then after the animals the woman. If Adam and Eve had endured for only one generation prior to the fall, they would not have fallen" [there is a question mark here in the notes]. Elsewhere, Anne Catherine says: "Adam was not created in paradise, but out of the earth, and then placed therein, at which time the animals were already present there. Eve was not yet present when he named them. The animals he named followed him [later] to the earth."

by the lance—God drew Eve.[1] I saw her small and delicate. But she quickly increased in size until full-grown. She was exquisitely beautiful. Were it not for the fall, all would be born in the same way, in tranquil slumber.

The hill opened, and at Adam's side arose a crystalline rock, formed apparently of precious stones; at Eve's side lay a white valley covered with something like fine white pollen, which lay closer by the Tree of Knowledge.

When Eve had been formed, I saw that God gave something, or allowed something, to flow upon Adam. This is impossible to describe. All I can say is that it was as if there streamed from the Godhead—apparently in human form—currents of light from forehead, mouth, breast, and hands. They united into a globe of light, in form somewhat like a bean, which entered Adam's right side, whence Eve had been taken. Adam alone received it, and as it seemed to me, this was the Germ of God's Blessing, which was *threefold*. The Blessing that Abraham received from the angel was *one*. It was of similar form, but not so luminous. It is so difficult to describe such holy things.[2]

Eve rose up before Adam, and he gave her his hand. She had beautiful blonde hair. They were like two unspeakably noble and beautiful children, perfectly luminous, and clothed with beams

---

[1] Elsewhere Anne Catherine says: "The woman was in Adam, in the figure I had seen in his right side when he was in the virgin earth, at the time God created him. And Adam yearned for her."

[2] On another occasion Anne Catherine suddenly passed into a vision that she could not express clearly. She had been preoccupied with the follies of her sister, and as she was speaking of this, all of a sudden she entered into a profound vision regarding the origin of evil and the separation of the sexes. But instead of remaining firmly within this vision, she seemed to be partly there, partly in the present moment, and somewhat confused. About four minutes passed in this, way, and then she said: "I was looking into paradise and beheld all the animals called forth in pairs, and how Adam saw that all was good—and that was *One*, Unity, which is a good number. Then I saw the figure of Eve coming out from Adam, and how she went with the serpent and stood beneath the tree and looked thence upon Adam with desire—and she was *Two*, duality, which is a malevolent number, from which comes all evil. Then I saw God come between and punish Adam and Even—and that was *Three*, a

of light as with a veil. I saw them as man and woman, yet not outwardly so. Eve had no breasts that I could see, nor what sometimes mars the outward form of even the most beautiful women,
such as over-broad hips or bent legs. There was nothing on or in
either of them that might serve sinful purposes. It was a great joy,
a pure happiness, to look upon them. They were all shining, and
as though clad in a glittering garment. They were indeed naked,
but without sin, or the means to sin. Their beauty was inexpressible. Eve was a little smaller and more delicate than Adam. I can
find no words to describe how repugnant and malformed our
contemporaries are compared to them.

From Adam's mouth I saw issuing a broad stream of glittering
light, and upon his forehead was an expression of great majesty.
Around his mouth played a sunbeam, but there was none around
Eve's. I saw Adam's heart very much the same as in men of the
present day, but his breast was surrounded by rays of light. In the
middle of his heart I saw a sparkling halo of glory. In it was a tiny
figure, as if holding something in its hand. I think it symbolized
the Third Person of the Godhead.[1] From the hands and feet of
Adam and Eve shot rays of light. Their hair fell in five glittering

---

benevolent number. *Four*, however, is confusion, and all was desolate, though I
did see how Noah led all creatures pair-by-pair into the ark. I don't recall this
part so well, but in some way the number four was not good. But *Five* was
again a beneficent number—I saw springs, like heavenly bodies, pouring
themselves forth from the surrounding air, flowing hither and yon. *Six* was a
good number also—I saw palm trees arising along rivers. But when I came to
the number *Seven* I came to a standstill in the vision." [Before adding this, she
said: "We are the Seven."] How is it that a vision such as this can so abruptly
come to her, so that she can scarcely find words to express it? And yet according to her, such visions come often. She calls them "profound thoughts." In
such wise does she perceive the consequences of evil, and such things.

[1] Immediately following in the notes is the following passage, which does
not seem to provide a full picture of the "child figure" referred to: "Threads
of light rayed out from the bottom of [Eve's] heart, ending in a radiant gar-
land beneath which in turn I saw a child, first small, then larger. The child
grew in the mother, and was from the beginning fully conscious, but then
emerged in a somnolent state from the mother's side, as had Eve from that of
Adam."

tresses, two from the temples, two behind the ears, and one from the back of the head.[1]

I have always thought that by the wounds of Jesus there were opened anew in the human body portals closed by Adam's sin. I have been given to understand that Longinus opened in Jesus's side the gate of regeneration to Eternal Life; and that no one entered heaven while that gate was closed; but such things are impossible to express.[2]

The glittering beams on Adam's head denoted his abundant fruitfulness, his glory, his connection with other radiations. And all this shining beauty is restored to glorified souls and bodies. Our hair is the ruined, the extinct glory; and as is this hair of ours to rays of light, so is our present flesh to that of Adam before the fall. The sunbeams around Adam's mouth bore reference to a holy posterity from God, which, had it not been for the fall, would have been effectuated by the spoken word. Such beams around Eve's mouth I did not see. Neither did I see stomach or ingestion such as we know. Fruits were enjoyed in the same way we now enjoy the sun and the moon—and they shimmered and shone. It was the fruit of the Forbidden Tree that first occasioned eating and reproduction—as we now know them—into the wholly inner and fallen workings of our bodies. Adam stretched forth his hand to Eve. They left the charming spot of Eve's creation and went through paradise, looking at everything, rejoicing in everything. That place was the highest in paradise. All was more radiant, more resplendent there than elsewhere.

---

[1] In a similar passage we read: "Before the fall, Adam and Eve appeared to me with a reddish glow. The region from their breast to their midriff was surrounded with rays, as with the radiance of blooming flowers. It seems to me, though I do not remember with complete clarity, that before Eve's creation, Adam bore her within himself, and that when she came out of his right side she was small but increased in size rapidly, so that soon she was standing alongside him. They were rather like palm trees, for in these trees the male and the female parts grow on separate branches."

[2] Elsewhere Anne Catherine says: "From the hands, feet, and breasts I saw streaming out rays of light. I have always seen that the wounds of Jesus were like portals of rebirth, and that none entered heaven until these wounds were opened. They are the portals of heaven."

The Tree of Life and the Tree of Knowledge

IN the center of the glittering garden I saw a sheet of water in which lay an island connected with the land opposite by a dam or pier. Both island and pier were covered with beautiful trees, but in the middle of the former stood one more magnificent than the others. It towered high above them as though guarding them. Its roots extended over the whole island as did also its branches, which were broad below and tapering to a point above. Its boughs were horizontal, and from them arose others like little trees. The leaves were fine, the fruit yellow and sessile in a leafy calyx like a budding rose. It was something like a cedar. I do not remember ever having seen Adam, Eve, or any animal near that tree on the island. But I saw beautiful noble-looking white birds and heard them singing in its branches. That tree was the Tree of Life.

Just before the pier that led to the island stood the Tree of Knowledge. The trunk was scaly like that of the palm. The leaves, which spread out directly from the stem, were very large and broad, in shape like the sole of a shoe. Hidden in the forepart of the leaves hung the fruit clustering in fives, one in front and four around the stem. The yellow fruit had something of the shape of an apple, though more of the nature of a pear or fig. It had five ribs uniting in a little cavity. It was pulpy like a fig inside, of the color of brown sugar, and streaked with blood-red veins. The tree was broader above than below, and its branches struck deep roots into the ground. I see a species of this tree still in warm countries. Its branches throw down shoots to the earth where they root and rise as new trunks. These in turn send forth branches, so that one such tree often covers a large tract of country. Whole families dwell under the dense foliage.

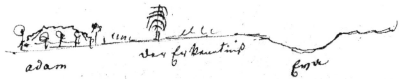

[The above rough sketch is taken from Brentano's notes]

At some distance to the right of the Tree of Knowledge I saw a small, oval, gently sloping hill of glittering red grains and all kinds of precious stones. It was terraced with crystals. Around it were slender trees just high enough to intercept the view. Plants and herbs grew around it, and they, like the trees, bore colored blossoms and nutritious fruits.

At some distance to the left of the Tree of Knowledge I saw a slope, a little dale. It looked like soft clay, or like mist, and it was covered with tiny white flowers and pollen. Here too were various kinds of vegetation, but all colorless, more like pollen than fruit.

It seemed as if these two—the hill and the dale—bore some reference to each other, as if the hill had been taken out of the dale, or as if something from the former was to be transplanted into the latter. They were to each other what the seed is to the field. Both seemed to me holy, and I saw that both—but especially the hill—shone with light. Between them and the Tree of Knowledge arose different kinds of trees and bushes. They were all, like everything else in nature, transparent, as if formed of light.

These two places were the abodes of our first parents. The Tree of Knowledge separated them. I think that God, after the creation of Eve, pointed out those places to them. I saw that Adam and Eve were little together at first. I saw them perfectly free from passion, each going about in a separate abode.

The animals were indescribably noble-looking and resplendent, and they served Adam and Eve. All had, according to their kind, certain retreats, abodes, and walks apart. The different spheres contained in themselves some great mystery of the divine law, and all were connected one with another. I saw far fewer animal types than exist today, but among these were some no longer to be found. Neither vine nor grain did I see in paradise.

The Fall

I SAW Adam and Eve walking through paradise for the first time. I saw a beautiful, smooth tree with wide-spreading branches that seemed to be their habitation. They wandered around rather like farmers surveying their fields. All was most pleasing to them. The animals were friendly toward them, ever trotting up and accompanying them on their way, though they appeared to be more familiar with Eve than with Adam. Eve was in fact more taken up with the earth and created things. She glanced below and around more frequently than Adam. She appeared the more inquisitive of the two. Adam was more silent, more absorbed in God.

Among the animals was one that followed Eve more closely than the others. It was a singularly gentle and winning, though artful creature. It was ever bringing them things, clearing each and every stone from their path, providing them with this and that. It seemed to be everywhere, offering them whatever they might desire. I know of none other to which I might compare it. It was slender and glossy, and it looked as if it had no bones. It walked upright on its short hind feet, its pointed tail trailing on the ground. Near the head, which was round with a face exceedingly shrewd, it had little short paws, and its wily tongue was ever in motion. The color of the neck, breast, and underpart of the body was pale yellow, and down the back it was a mottled brown very much the same as an eel. It was about as tall as a child of ten years. It was constantly around Eve, and so coaxing and intelligent, so nimble and supple, that she took great delight in it. But to me there was something horrible about it. I can see it distinctly even now. I never saw it touch either Adam or Eve. Before the fall, the distance between humankind and the lower animals was great, and I never saw the first human beings touch any of them. They had, it is true, more confidence in man, but they kept at a certain distance from him.[1]

When Adam and Eve returned to the region of shining light, a radiant figure like a majestic man with glittering silver hair stood

---

[1] Anne Catherine's simplicity, her innocence of any real instruction with respect to what holy scripture might otherwise have provided her, comes into

before them. He pointed around, and in few words appeared to be giving all things over to them and to be commanding them something. They did not look intimidated, but listened to him naturally. When he vanished, they appeared more satisfied, more happy. They appeared to understand things better, to find more order in things, for now they felt gratitude—but Adam more than Eve. She thought more of their actual bliss and of the things around them than of giving thanks for them. She did not rest in God so perfectly as did Adam; her soul was more taken up with created things.

I think Adam and Eve went around paradise three times. However, I did not see them touch each other, other than when Adam first awoke and upon seeing Eve took her by the hand. At first they seemed to me somewhat dull or slow, but were now happier, lighter, for they were thankful—Adam however rather more than Eve, who felt more a sense of good fortune with regard to the things around her than gratitude. She was not as present in God as was Adam, but more with nature in her soul. The animals grew ever more pleasing and tame.

Again I saw Adam on the shining hill upon which God had formed the woman from a rib of his side as he lay buried in sleep. He stood alone under the trees lost in gratitude and wonder. I saw Eve near the Tree of Knowledge, as if about to pass it, and with her that same animal, more wily and sportive than ever. Eve was charmed with the serpent; she took great delight in it. It ran up the Tree of Knowledge until its head was on a line with hers. Then, clinging to the trunk with its hind feet, it moved its head toward hers and told her that, if she would eat of the fruit of that tree, she would no longer be in servitude, she would become free and understand how the multiplication of the human race was to

strikingly clear evidence here, for she continued to maintain that what she saw was no ordinary serpent, but the upright moving, four-footed creature depicted above, which with loathing and a shuddering aversion she regarded as the tool of the temptation.

be effected. Adam and Eve had already received the command to increase and multiply, but I understood that they did not know as yet how God willed it to be brought about. I saw too that, had they known it and yet sinned after that knowledge, redemption would not have been possible.

Eve now became more thoughtful. She appeared to be moved by desire for what the serpent had promised. Something degrading took possession of her. It made me feel anxious. She glanced toward Adam, who was still quietly standing under the trees. She called him, and he came. Eve started to meet him, but turned back. There was a restlessness, a hesitancy, about her movements. Again she started, as if intending to pass the tree, but once more hesitated, approached it from the left, and stood behind it, screened by its long, hanging leaves. The tree was broader above than below, and its wide, leafy branches drooped to the ground. Just within Eve's reach hung a remarkably fine bunch of fruit.

And now Adam approached. Eve caught him by the arm and pointed to the talking animal, and he listened to its words. When Eve laid her hand on Adam's arm, she touched him for the first time. He did not touch her, but the splendor around them grew dim. I saw the animal pointing to the fruit, but he did not venture to snap it off for Eve. But when the longing for it arose in her heart, he broke off and handed her the central and most beautiful piece of the clustering five.

And now I saw Eve draw near to Adam and offer him the fruit. Had he refused it, sin would not have been committed. I saw the fruit break, as it were, in Adam's hand. He saw pictures in it, and it was as if he and Eve were instructed upon what they should not have known. The interior of the fruit was blood-red and full of veins. I saw Adam and Eve losing their brilliancy and diminishing in stature—they became to some degree animalistic. It was as if the sun went down. The animal glided down the tree, and I saw it running off for the first time on all fours. I did not see the fruit taken into the mouth as we now take food in eating, but it disappeared between Adam and Eve. Then, as they departed, it seemed to me now that they were naked, and that from that moment on the sun commenced to recede.

I saw that while the serpent was still in the tree, Eve sinned, for her consent was with the temptation. I learned also at that moment what I cannot clearly repeat; namely, that the serpent was as it were, in form and figure, the embodiment of Adam and Eve's will, a being by which they could do all things, could attain all things. Here it was that satan entered. I saw that Eve fell already into sin simply by virtue of the fact that as the serpent sat upon the tree, her own will was already incorporated therein.

Sin was not completed by eating the forbidden fruit. But that fruit from the tree which, rooting its branches in the earth thus sent out new shoots—and which continued to do the same after the fall—conveyed the idea of a more absolute propagation, a sensual implanting in self at the cost of separation from God. So along with disobedience there sprang from their indulgence that severing of the creature from God, that planting in self and through self, and those selfish passions in human nature. One that uses the fruit solely for the enjoyment it affords must accept as the consequence of the act the subversion, the debasement, of nature, as well as sin and death.

The Blessing of a pure and holy multiplying out of God and by God, which Adam had received after the creation of Eve, was in consequence of that indulgence withdrawn from him; for I saw that the instant Adam left his hill to go to Eve, the Lord grasped him in the back and took Something from him. From that Something, I felt that the world's salvation would come.

Once on the feast of the holy and immaculate conception God gave me a vision of that mystery. I saw enclosed in Adam and Eve the corporal and spiritual life of all humankind. I saw that by the fall it became corrupted, mixed up with evil, and that the bad angels had acquired power over it. I saw the Second Person of the Godhead come down and, with something like a crooked blade, take the Blessing from Adam before he had sinned. At the same instant I saw the Virgin issuing from Adam's side like a little luminous cloud, and soaring all resplendent up to God.

By the reception of the fruit, Adam and Eve became as it were intoxicated, and their consent to sin wrought in them a great change. It was the serpent in them. Its nature pervaded theirs, and then came the tares among the wheat.

As punishment and reparation, circumcision was instituted. As

41

the vine is pruned, that it may not run rampant, may not become sour and unfruitful, so must it be done to humankind, that they may regain their lost perfection. Once, when the reparation of the fall was shown me in symbolical pictures, I saw Eve in the act of issuing from Adam's side, and even then stretching out her neck after the forbidden fruit. She ran quickly to the tree and clasped it in her arms. In a reciprocal picture I saw Jesus born of the immaculate Virgin. He ran straight to the cross and embraced it. I saw posterity obscured and ruined by Eve, but again purified by the passion of Jesus. By the pains of penance must the evil love of self be rooted out of the flesh. The word of the Epistle that the son of the handmaid shall not be joint heir, I always understood to mean the flesh and slavish subjection thereto, typified under the figure of the handmaid. Marriage is a state of penance. It calls for prayer, fasting, alms-deeds, renunciation, and the intention to increase the kingdom of God.

Adam and Eve before sin were very differently constituted from what we poor, miserable creatures now are. There was nothing shameful about them, no complex of ever-conflicting inner organs, such as came to be later. With the reception of the forbidden fruit they admitted into themselves a power of reproduction, of becoming form or thing, such that what previously had been of spirit became now flesh and bone—all grew to be [material] things, instruments, vessels.[1] At first they were one in God, they sought self in God; but afterward they stood apart from God in their own will. And this self-will is self-seeking, a lusting after sin and impurity. By eating the forbidden fruit man turned away from his Creator. It was as if he drew creation into himself. All creative power, operations, and attributes, their commingling with one another and with all nature, became in man material things of different forms and functions.

Once man was endowed with the kingship of nature, but now all in him has *become* nature. He is now one of its slaves, a master conquered and fettered. He must now struggle and fight with

---

[1] The preceding sentences are not Anne Catherine's word-for-word, for her expressions were unclear and seemingly confused; what is written here, however, is the only possible meaning that can be drawn from them. CB

nature—but I cannot clearly express it. It was as if man once possessed all things in God, their Creator and their Center; but now he made *himself* their center, and they became his *master*.

I saw the interior—the organs of humankind, as if in the flesh—as corporeal, corruptible images of creatures, as well as their relations with one another, from the stars down to the tiniest living thing. All exert an influence on man. He is connected with all of them; he must act and struggle against them, and from them suffer. But I cannot express it clearly since I too am a member of the fallen race.

However this I much I do know, that in the [original] holy bodies there was no gender such as we know them. Our blood is a consequence of the fall, as is the frailty of woman, which must be acknowledged and then transformed through humility into godliness. In truly pious, guiltless, holy individuals we find no trace of [baser] sexual characteristics such as we do in the sinful and impure—in whom it may become an abomination. When I wish to confess and find myself obliged to struggle with self-exoneration and the indictment of others—that is when I come to feel my own entrails and the blood coursing through my veins.[1]

I had a great, indescribable vision of sin, the reparation through Jesus, and the state of the priesthood, and I understood how with infinite toil and pains all that is spoiled, destroyed, or lost must be restored and turned again into the way of salvation. I have had an

---

[1] Elsewhere Anne Catherine says: "I recall as a child feeling sad and ashamed regarding our human origins, and beholding in vision Eve as she would have been, but for the fall into sin. Her body was entirely different. I saw no sign of such entrails and invaginations as we now possess. I recall seeing a heart, and stemming from it many vessels that formed into a round ball sunk in upon itself, under which lay a child, arms crossed upon its breast and head pressed against Eve's right side beneath the ribs of her chest. Is saw it grow and swell in exactly the same place whence Eve arose out of Adam, and where Longinus pierced the side of Christ Jesus. There I saw the skin part, though without pain, and the child come forth from the wound as though through pure lips. The child was not nourished by its mother through an umbilical cord, but through a tube that covered its lips with a slight enfolding. Neither could it have been nursed by its mother, for upon her breast I saw no nipples. I believe conception was accomplished then with neither consciousness nor fleshly conjoining—but by means of the Word alone."

immense, connected vision of the fall and redemption. It would take a year to relate it, for I saw and understood all mysteries clearly and distinctly; but I cannot fully explain it.

I was traveling an allegorical path toward a great house,[1] and I saw in its numerous apartments all forms of sin and preparation. I saw sin from the fall of the angels and Adam down to the present, in its numberless ramifications, and at the same time I beheld all the preparations for its reparation to the coming of Jesus and his death on the cross. I saw his power transmitted to priests in what related to the remedy, and how every Christian shares in Jesus Christ. I saw the imperfections, the decay of the priesthood, and their cause, also the chastisements awaiting them and the efficacy of expiatory sufferings, and I felt by my pains the strict bond existing between the fault and its atonement. I saw a future war, many dangers and sufferings in store for me.

All these varied instructions and revelations of history, nature, and the mysteries of God's kingdom upon earth, appeared to me in perfect order, following one another, arising from one another clearly and intelligibly. All were explained to me in parables of labor and tasks, while suffering, satisfaction, and reparation were shown me under the form of sewing. I have had to rip out others' work, as well as my own, and do it over with great pains and trouble. I had to examine what was crooked, see how it had happened, and patiently fix it straight. In the shape of different articles, in the various kinds of sewing, in the trimming, and the careless way in which it was all done, I saw the origin and consequence of every sin; in the repairing of it I saw the effect of spiritual suffering and labor in prayer. I recognized work belonging to deceased persons, my former acquaintances, work that had actually been done and that was now brought to me to do over again. I had also to rip out some of my own sewing: for example an undergarment I had embroidered too richly to gratify a vain woman, and other things of the kind; but my work for the Church and the poor was good.

I went into the nuptial house as if to a school, and there my Spouse explained everything to me, showing me in great historical pictures all he had done to repair the sin of Adam. I saw all as

---

[1] Identified below as the house of the Bridegroom, or nuptial house.

going on under my eyes; and yet at the same time it seemed as if I beheld it in a mirror, which mirror was myself.[1]

My Affianced explained to me how all things had deteriorated since the fall, how all had become impure. When the angels fell, innumerable bad spirits came upon the earth and filled the air. I saw many things infected by their malice, and possessed by them in various ways.

The first man was like heaven. He was an image of God. In him was unity and his form was a reproduction of the divine Prototype. He was to receive and enjoy creatures, accepting them from God and returning thanks for them. He was free, and therefore was he subjected to trial.

The garden of Eden with all it contained was a perfect picture of the kingdom of God. So too was the Tree of Knowledge. Its fruit, on account of its essence, its properties, and effects, was not to be eaten by man since he would thereby become an independent being, having his principle of action in himself; he would abandon God to concentrate himself in himself, so that the finite would compass the infinite; therefore was he forbidden to eat its fruit—I cannot explain how I saw this.

At first all was in balance and even. But when the shining hill upon which Adam stood in paradise arose, when was hollowed out the bright flowering vale in which I beheld Eve, the corrupter was already near.

After the fall, all was changed, divided, dispersed; what had been one became many, creatures looked no longer to God alone, each was concentrated in self. At first there were two, they increased to three, and finally to an infinite number. They wanted to be one like unto God, but they became a multitude. Separating from God, they reproduced themselves in infinite varieties. From images of God they became images of themselves, bearing the

---

[1] Of such matters Anne Catherine sometimes reports so little only because she cannot dedicate to them sufficient time or earnest endeavor; for the pilgrim can never concede that what is given her in spiritual forms is entirely inexpressible. Of what she received on this occasion we give here what little she was able to retain—rather like particles of feather dust fallen from a great, many-colored bird. CB

likeness of sin. They entered into communication with the fallen angels; they participated in the fruits of the earth already tainted by these spirits. This indiscriminate blending of things, this division in humankind and fallen nature gave birth to endless sins and miseries.

My Spouse showed me all this clearly, distinctly, intelligibly, more clearly than one sees the ordinary things of life. I thought at the time that a child might comprehend it, but now I am unable to repeat it.

I saw that but for the fall, conception and birth would not have been accompanied by humiliation and pain. Likewise it was the fall that gave rise to subversion and degradation, not only in human nature but in all of nature. In the wake of sin came the foundering of human nature and the first outward manifestations of sexual differences. Shame in face of these changes as punishment and consequence of sin led to an involution and transformation of the human body's inner organization, which in turn expressed itself in the pain of childbirth.

The form of fruits at that time revealed their essence and significance; and to consume them meant to imbibe directly their inner content or concept. There was no mechanical chewing or chemical breakdown, assimilation, and excretion. The forbidden fruit, however, I saw as a tree that sent its branches down into the earth, whence they grew forth again anew (this remained true also after the fall), filled now with a self-enclosed power of propagation, a sensual implanting within itself that separated it from God. Consumption of this fruit led to disobedience, to creaturely separation from God, and the establishment in human nature—in self and through self—of desire. This forbidden desire led to forgetfullness of the inner essence of the fruit and thereby to an incapacity to assimilate it. The consequence of this was the arising of the difference between the sexes, a defection of nature, and an abasement of conception and birth leading to sin and death.

The Promise of the Redeemer

AFTER the fall of humankind, as has been said, God made known to the angels His plan for the restoration of the human race. I saw the throne of God. I saw the Holy Trinity and a movement in the divine Persons. I saw the nine choirs of angels and God announcing to them the way by which He would restore the fallen race. I saw the inexpressible joy and jubilation of the angels at the announcement.

I saw Adam's glittering rock of precious stones arise before the throne of God, as if borne up by angels. It had steps cut in it, it increased in size, it became a throne, a tower, and it extended on all sides until it embraced all things. I saw the nine choirs of angels around it, and above the angels in heaven I saw the image of the Virgin. It was not Mary in time; it was Mary in eternity, Mary in God.[1] The Virgin entered the tower, which opened to receive her, and she appeared to become one with it. Then I saw issuing from the Holy Trinity an apparition which likewise went into the tower.

Among the angels I noticed a kind of monstrance at which all were working. It was in shape like a tower, and on it were all kinds of mysterious carving. Near it on either side stood two figures, their joined hands embracing it. At every instant it became larger and more magnificent. I saw Something from God passing through the angelic choirs and going into the monstrance. It was a shining Holy Thing, and it became more clearly defined the nearer it drew to the monstrance. It appeared to me to be the Germ of the divine Blessing for a pure offspring that had been given to Adam but withdrawn when he was on the point of hearkening to Eve and consenting to eat the forbidden fruit. It was the Blessing that was again bestowed upon Abraham, withdrawn from Jacob, by Moses deposited in the Ark of the Covenant, and lastly received by Joachim, the father of Mary, in order that Mary might be as pure and stainless in her conception as was Eve upon coming forth from the side of the sleeping Adam. The monstrance, likewise, went into the tower.

[1] See "The Eternal Mary" in *The Life of the Virgin Mary.*

I saw too a chalice prepared by the angels. It was of the same shape as that used at the Last Supper, and it also went into the tower. To the right of the tower I saw, as if on the edge of a golden cloud, grapevines and wheat intertwining like the fingers of clasped hands. From them sprang a branch, a whole genealogical tree, upon whose boughs were little figures of males and females reaching hands to one another. Its highest blossom was the crib with the child.

Then I saw in pictures the mystery of redemption from the Promise down to the fullness of time; and in side pictures I saw *counteracting influences* at work. At last, over the shining rock, I saw a large and magnificent Church. It was the one, holy, Catholic Church, which bears living in itself the salvation of the whole world. The connection of these pictures one with another, and their transition from one to another, was wonderful. Even what was evil and opposed to the end in view, even what was rejected by the angels as unfit, was made subservient to the development of redemption. And so I saw the ancient temple rising from below; it was very large and like a Church but it had no tower. It was pushed to one side by the angels, and there it stood slanting. I saw a great mussel shell make its appearance and try to force its way into the old temple, but it too was hurried aside.

I saw appear a broad, lopped-off tower through whose numerous gateways figures like Abraham and the children of Israel entered—it was significant of their bondage in Egypt. It was shoved aside, as well as another Egyptian tower in staircase form. The latter was symbolical of astrology and soothsaying. Then appeared an Egyptian temple. It was pushed aside like the others and remained standing crooked.

At last I saw a vision, on earth, such as God had shown to Adam—that is, that a Virgin would arise and restore to him the salvation he had forfeited. Adam knew not when it would take place and I saw his deep sadness because Eve bore him only sons. But at last she bore a daughter.

I saw Noah and his sacrifice at the time in which he received from God the Blessing. Then I had visions of Abraham, of his Blessing, and of the Promise of a son Isaac. I saw the Blessing descending from firstborn to firstborn, and always transmitted with a sacramental action. I saw Moses on the night of Israel's departure from Egypt getting possession of the Mystery, the Holy Thing, of which none other knew save Aaron.[1] I saw it afterward in the Ark of the Covenant. Only the high priests and certain saints, by a revelation from God, had any knowledge of it. I saw the transmitting of this Mystery through the ancestry of Jesus Christ down to Joachim and Anne, the purest and holiest couple that ever existed, and from whom was born Mary, the spotless Virgin. And then I saw Mary becoming the *living* Ark of God's Covenant.

The Trinity and the Plan of Redemption

A GREAT mystery was enacted in heaven: that of the decision, made in accordance with the counsel of the Holy Trinity, to redeem humankind. This mystery is now celebrated in the highest heaven as a great festival of remembrance. O, how indescribably beautiful it is! If only my father confessor were here! I have such a wonder to tell him.[2]

I have seen much about a festival in heaven regarding the Holy Trinity's decree in favor of redeeming humankind. Only the Holy Trinity was present, along with angels of many kinds, though I did see also all manner of images, figures, and combinations thereof. But then I was impeded and thereby confounded. However I saw

---

[1] See "Moses" and "The Ark of the Covenant" in *Mysteries of the Old Testament*.

[2] The pilgrim said to Anne Catherine that she might at least tell him, but at this a sort of hesitation came over her, and she could not continue. The following day she addressed this hesitation somewhat, saying that though she knew not how or why she would sometimes fall into a sort of restraint or perplexity, and suddenly, when she wanted to relate something she had seen in vision, she draw up short, unable to go further. This is how it had been the preceding day regarding the Festival of the Holy Trinity. It was as though she had suddenly been prohibited from speaking further, after which all fell into confusion. Unfortunately many scenes from Anne Catherine's visions went missing in this way. She had always on the one hand a divine injunction to see and report what came to her, but on the other the private charge of her father confessor to the contrary—so that she was suspended as it were between ordered certainty and opinion.

come forth a kernel of wheat and a small sprig of the vine of the grape. And the angelic beings brought trees and shrubs of all kinds, together with the most wonderful fruits and flowers. I understood that these pure fruits represented redemption. In this was the whole mystery of bread and wine prefigured. It was beyond describing, and I was frustrated in my ability to do so.

The pilgrim said to her: "When I asked you yesterday whether or not the plan for redemption had not already been established prior to the Creation, you said 'that lay still in the balance.'" And to this Anne Catherine replied: "Yes, I beheld this image of the balance, but I cannot now recall it clearly, and so am reluctant to speak of it."[1]

She continued: I saw a great figure, an angel or some other power standing astride two spheres, two worlds. The figure was holding a balance, one of whose pans was round and the other compressed into a shape like that of a ship, and from the latter something was flowing. Then from the Holy Trinity came forth one of the Persons thereof, as though from the Heart or Breast of the Trinity. It was a Word, but also a Form. I saw unfold a great series of such occurrences, but can no longer call them forth clearly. At the time the scene was clear and precise, but I find myself more and more anxious about describing such things, and related temptations.

I saw how in the great deluge all humankind was destroyed, and how Noah then received the seed of wheat and the sprig of the vine. The seed he ate, and the sprig he planted. The latter was however more primitive, less cultivated—not at all the same as what Abraham later received. It was more like a simple foodstuff, or remedial plant. What Abraham received had more of spirit and power; it was bread and flesh, wine and blood.

Adam and Eve Driven from Paradise

AFTER some time I saw Adam and Eve wandering about in great distress. They were no longer beaming with light and they went

---

[1] At this I became anxious that by pressing her in this way she might be unable to speak further on the subject in any detail.

about, one here, the other there, as if seeking something they had lost. They were ashamed of each other. Every step they took led them downward, as if the ground gave way beneath their feet. They carried gloom wherever they went; the plants lost their bright colors and turned gray, and the animals fled before them. They sought large leaves and wove them into a cincture for their loins. They always wandered about separate.

After they had thus fled for a considerable time, the region of refulgent light whence they had come began to look like the summit of a distant mountain. Among the bushes of a gloomy-looking plain they hid themselves, but apart. Then a voice from above called them, but they would not obey the call. They were frightened, they fled still further and hid still deeper among the bushes. It made me sad to see that. But the voice became more imperative, and in spite of their desire to flee and hide they were compelled to come forth.

The majestic figure shining with light again appeared. Adam and Eve with bowed head stepped from their hiding places but they dared not look upon their Lord. They glanced at each other and both acknowledged their guilt. And now God pointed out to them a plain still lower than the one on which they stood. On it were bushes and trees. On reaching it, they became humble and for the first time rightly understood their miserable condition. I saw them praying when left there alone. They separated, fell on their knees, and raised up their hands with tears and cries. I thought as I gazed upon them how good it is to be alone in prayer. Adam and Eve were at this time clothed in a garment that reached from the shoulders to the knee and that was girded at the waist by a strip of the inner bark of a tree.

There is something else to say about the form of our first parents. Before the fall I saw them in human form, with countenance, hands, and feet—but as lacking both navel and nipples.[1]

While our first parents were descending lower and lower from

---

[1] In the notes at this point is the following: "Was their immortal body, then, laid aside like a garment, or did these other features appear only after the fall?"

the place of their creation, paradise itself appeared—like a cloud
—to be mounting higher and higher above them. Then a fiery
ring, like the circle sometimes seen around the sun and moon,
came down from heaven and settled around the height upon
which was paradise.

Adam and Eve had been only one day in paradise. I now see
paradise far, far off like a strip of land directly under the point of
sunrise. When the sun rises, it mounts up from the right of that
strip of land which lies east of the prophet mountain and just
where the sun rises. It looks to me like an egg hanging over indescribably clear water that separates it from the earth. The prophet
mountain is, as it were, a promontory rising up through that
water. On that mountain one sees extraordinarily verdant regions
broken here and there by deep abysses and ravines full of water. I
have indeed seen people climbing up the prophet mountain, but
they did not go far.

I saw Adam and Eve reach the earth, their place of penance.
Oh, what a touching sight—those two creatures expiating their
fault upon the naked earth! Adam had been allowed to bring an
olive branch with him from paradise, and now he planted it.
Later on the cross was made from its wood. Adam and Eve were
unspeakably sad. Where I saw them, they could scarcely get a
glimpse of paradise, and they were constantly descending lower
and lower. It seemed as if something revolved, and they came at
last—through night and darkness—to the wretched, miserable
place upon which they had to do penance.

The Family of Adam

IT was to the region of the Mount of Olives that I saw Adam and
Eve come. The country was very different from what it is at
present, but I was assured it was the same. I saw Adam and Eve
living and doing penance on that part of the Mount of Olives
upon which Jesus sweat blood. They cultivated the soil. I saw
them surrounded by sons. They were in great distress and they
implored God to bestow upon them a daughter, for they had
received the Promise that the woman's seed should crush the serpent's head.

Eve bore children at stated intervals.[1] After each birth a number of years was always devoted to penance. It was after seven years of penance that Seth, the Child of Promise, was born of Eve in the grotto of the crib, where also an angel announced to Eve that Seth was the Seed given her by God in the place of Abel. For a long time Seth was concealed in that grotto, likewise in the cave in which Abraham was afterward suckled, for his brothers, like those of Joseph, sought his life.[2]

Once I saw about twelve people: Adam, Eve, Cain, Abel, two sisters, and some young children. All were clothed in skins thrown over their shoulders like a scapular and girded at the waist. The female dress was large and full around the breast where it served as a pocket. It fell down around the limbs, and was fastened at the sides and once under the arm. The men wore shorter dresses, which had a pocket fastened to them. The skins from which their dresses were made were, from the neck to the elbow, exceedingly fine and white. They all looked very noble and beautiful in their clothing. They had huts in those days, partly sunk in the earth and covered with plants. Their household was quite well-arranged. I saw orchards of low but tolerably vigorous fruit trees. There was grain also, such as wheat, which God had given to Adam for seed.

I do not remember having seen either grapevines or wheat in paradise. None of the productions of paradise had to be prepared for eating. Such preparation is a consequence of sin and, therefore, a symbol of labor and suffering. God gave to Adam whatever it was necessary for him to sow. I remember having seen men who looked like angels taking something to Noah when he went

---

[1] Elsewhere we read: "I must say, for I always see it so, that the children of Shem, Ham, and Japhet all went into the ark. There were many little boys and girls in it—in fact all of Noah's family that were good. holy scripture mentions only three of Adam's children—Cain, Abel, and Seth—and yet I see many others among them and I always see them in pairs, boys and girls."

[2] Elsewhere also: "Abraham's early childhood was similar to that which occurred to the child Moses when his nurse saved his life. It had been prophesied to the ruler of the country that a wonderful child would be born, whose birth would be very fatal to his interests. The ruler took measures accordingly, on which account Abraham's mother concealed herself before his birth in the same cave in which Seth had been hidden by Eve."

into the ark. It appeared to me to be a vine branch stuck in an apple.

A certain kind of grain grew wild at that time, and among it Adam had to sow the good wheat. That improved it for awhile but it again degenerated and became worse and worse. The wild grain was excellent in those early times. It was most luxuriant further to the east, in India or China, where as yet there were but few inhabitants. It does not thrive where wine is largely made and fish abound.[1]

The milk of animals was drunk in those days, and they likewise ate cheese dried in the sun. Among the animals I noticed sheep in particular. All that Adam had named followed him from paradise, but afterward they fled from him. He had to entice them back with food—that is, the domestic animals—and familiarize them to himself. I saw birds hopping about, little animals running around, and all sorts of bounding creatures,[2] such as antelopes and deer.

The household order was quite patriarchal. I saw Adam's children in their separate huts, reclining around a stone at meals. I saw them also praying and giving thanks.

God had taught Adam to offer sacrifice; he was the priest in his family. Cain and Abel also were priests. I saw that even the preparations for their sacrifice took place in a separate hut. On the head they wore caps made of leaves with their stalks woven together. They were shaped like a ship and had a rim in front by which they could be raised from the head.

Those first human beings had beautiful skin of a yellowish tinge, which shone like silk, and their hair was reddish-yellow like

[1] The full passage regarding this subject reads as follows: "A wild grain (or better said, type of grass) grew there also, among which Adam had to sow the nobler seed, which in turn improved the wild. The latter however would ever and again revert to type, all to the worse. In the earliest time this wild species of grain grew especially well and high toward the East, in India and China, at a time when those regions were less populated. But such was not the case in places where grapes grew, or fish thrived [this last sentence is underlined in the notes, as of unclear meaning]."

[2] In the notes we find alongside the expression *little animals* the query "hares?" and next to *bounding creatures* "kangaroos?"

gold. Adam wore his hair long. His beard was short at first but later he let it grow. Eve at first wore her long hair hanging around her, but later she wound it around her head in two coils like a cap.[1] At the beginning she wore a skirt of leaves and around her breast and midriff garlands or windings thereof as well.

Fire I always saw like a hidden flame that appeared to be in the earth. It was given to humankind from heaven, and God Himself taught the use of it. They burned for fuel a yellow substance that looked like earth. I saw no cooking going on. In the beginning the food was merely dried in the sun and the wheat after being crushed was exposed under twisted covers to the sun's heat to dry. God gave them wheat, barley, and rye, and taught them how to cultivate them. He guided humankind in all things.

I saw no large rivers in the beginning as, for instance, the Jordan; but fountains sprang forth whose waters were conducted into reservoirs. Along with the waters came fish, and also with the rain.[2] These were very small at first but then bred larger. Originally all the animals were very shy. Adam had to coax and feed them in order to gather them to him.

Flesh meat was not eaten before Abel's death.

I once had a vision of Mount Golgotha. I saw on it a prophet, the companion of Elijah. The Mount was at that time full of caves and sepulchers. The prophet entered one of the caves and from a stone coffin filled with bones took up the skull of Adam. Instantly an angel appeared before him, saying: "That is Adam's skull," and forbade its removal. Scattered over the skull was some thin yellow hair. From the prophet's account of what had occurred, the spot was named "the place of skull" (Golgotha).[3] Christ's cross stood in a straight line above that skull at the time of his crucifixion. I was interiorly instructed that the spot upon which the skull rests

---

[1] There follows here a note speculating whether there were three coils rather than two, such as Anne Catherine saw in the case of Mary.

[2] Here stands a question mark in the notes.

[3] *Golgotha* is the Greek term for the "place of the skull" (in Aramaic, *Gagulta*), later translated into Latin as *Calvariae Locus*, from which derives the word *Calvary.*

is the middle point of the earth. I was told the distance east, south, and west in numbers, but I have forgotten them.[1]

Rising out of an image of Adam's skull I beheld in brief paradise and the fall. I saw Adam arising out of the earth as from a Form; and the earth was a virgin. I then saw Eve arising from Adam's side; and Adam was virginal. As Eve thus arose she craned her neck toward the forbidden fruit and immediately thereafter hastened to the tree and embraced it. Then in a like but contrasting image I saw Jesus born of a Virgin and immediately hasten to the cross and embrace it.

On this occasion I was also given special insight into the recently received vision regarding the parable of the king and queen.[2] I saw that the place where their gardens came together, where rose aloft the tree upon which the differing fruits of the king and of the queen united and over which stood the heavenly table at which the two joined themselves together by sharing angelic bread, was no other than Mount Golgotha.

On the Name of Golgotha

WHILE meditating on the name of Golgotha, or Calvary, "the place of skulls," borne by the rock upon which Jesus was crucified, I became deeply absorbed in contemplation and beheld in spirit all ages from the time of Adam to that of Christ, and in this vision the origin of the name was made known to me. I here give all that I remember on this subject.

I saw Adam, after his expulsion from paradise, weeping in the grotto on the Mount of Olives where Jesus sweated blood and water. I saw how Seth was promised to Eve in the grotto of the manger at Bethlehem, and how she brought him forth in that same grotto. I also saw Eve living in some caverns near Hebron, where the Essene monastery of Mizpah was afterward established.

---

[1] Anne Catherine here adds: "I have also seen things in this way as from above; and then all is much clearer than when looking at a map, for I can see both near and far, and with equal resolution, each city, village, body of water, etc."

[2] See "A Wonderful Parable of Marriage" in *Inner Life and Worlds of Soul & Spirit*.

I then beheld the country where Jerusalem was built, as it appeared after the deluge, and the land was all unsettled, black, stony, and very different from what it had been before. At an immense depth below the rock that constitutes Golgotha, or Mount Calvary (which was formed in this spot by the rolling of the waters), I saw the tomb of Adam and Eve. The head and one rib were wanting to one of the skeletons, and the remaining head was placed within the same skeleton, to which it did not belong. The bones of Adam and Eve had not all been left in this grave, for Noah had some of them with him in the ark and they were transmitted from generation to generation by the patriarchs. Noah, and also Abraham, were in the habit, when offering sacrifice, of always laying some of Adam's bones upon the altar to remind the Almighty of His Promise. When Jacob gave Joseph his variegated robe he at the same time gave him some bones of Adam to be kept as relics. Joseph always wore them on his bosom and they were placed with his own bones in the first reliquary that the children of Israel brought out of Egypt. I have seen similar things, but some I have forgotten and the others time fails me to describe.

As regards the origin of the name of Golgotha, or Calvary, I here give all I know [as described similarly on page 55]. I beheld the mountain that bears this name as it was in the time of the prophet Elisha. It was not the same then as at the time of Our Lord's crucifixion, but was a hill with many walls and caverns, resembling tombs, upon it. I saw the prophet Elisha descend into these caverns (I cannot say whether in reality or only in a vision) and I saw him take out a skull from a stone sepulcher in which bones were resting. Someone who was by his side—I think an angel—said to him, "This is the skull of Adam." The prophet was desirous to take it away but his companion forbade him. I saw upon the skull some few hairs of a fair color.

I learned also that the prophet having related what had happened to him, the spot received the name of Golgotha. Finally I saw that the cross of Jesus was placed vertically over the skull of Adam. I was informed that this spot was the exact center of the earth; and at the same time I was shown the numbers and measures proper to every country, but I have forgotten them, individually as well as in general. Yet I have seen this center from above, and as it were from a bird's-eye view. In that way a person sees far more clearly than on a map all the different countries, mountains, deserts, seas, rivers, towns, and even the smallest places, whether distant or near at hand.

Cain • The Children of God • The Giants

I SAW that Cain conceived on the Mount of Olives the design to murder Abel. After the deed he wandered about the same spot frightened and distracted, planting trees and tearing them up again. Then I saw a majestic figure in the form of a man refulgent with light appear to him. "Cain," he said, "where is thy brother Abel?" Cain did not at first see the figure, but when he did he turned and answered: "I know not. He has not been given in charge to me." But when God replied that Abel's blood cried to him from the earth, Cain grew more troubled and I saw that he disputed long with God. God told him that he should be cursed upon the earth, that it should bring forth no fruit for him, and that he should forthwith flee from the land in which he then dwelt. Cain responded that everywhere his fellow men would seek to kill him.

There were already many people upon the earth. Cain was very old and had children. Abel also left children, and there were other brothers and sisters, the children of Adam. But God replied that it would not be so—that whoever should kill Cain should himself be punished sevenfold—and he placed a sign upon him that no one should slay him. Cain's posterity gradually became colored. Ham's children also were browner than those of Shem. They who were distinguished by a particular mark engendered children of the same stamp; and as corruption increased the mark also increased until at last it covered the whole body, and people became darker and darker. But yet in the beginning there were no people perfectly black; they became so only by degrees.

God pointed out to Cain a region to which he should flee. And because Cain said: "Then wilt thou let me starve?"—(the earth was for him accursed)—God answered no, that he should eat the flesh of animals. He told him likewise that a Nation would arise from him, and that good also would come from him. Before this, as it seemed to me, men ate no flesh. Cain went forth and built a city, which he named after his son Enoch.

Abel was slain in the valley of Jehosaphat opposite Mount Golgotha. Many murders and evil deeds took place there at a subsequent period. At a later time, after Christ's ascension, a disciple was brought here and martyred. Cain slew Abel with a kind of club that he used to break soft stones and earth when planting in the fields. The club must have been of hard stone, for it was shaped like a pickaxe, the handle of wood.

We must not picture to ourselves the earth before the deluge as it is now. Palestine was by no means so broken up by valleys and ravines. Plains were far more extensive and single mountains less lofty. The Mount of Olives was at that time only a gentle rising. The crib cave of Bethlehem was later a wild cavern, but the surroundings were different.

The people of those early times were larger, though not out of proportion. We would regard them with astonishment but not with fright, for they were far more beautiful in form than people of a later period—their joints, tendons, and musculature were more evident as compared to our time, when the human form is filled out, softer, and more rounded. Among the old marble statues that I see in many places lying in subterranean caves may be found similar figures.

Cain led his children and grandchildren to the region pointed out to him and there they separated.[1] Of Cain himself I have never seen anything more that was sinful. His punishment appeared to consist in hard, but fruitless labor. Nothing in which he was personally engaged succeeded. I saw that he was mocked and reviled by his children and grandchildren, treated badly in every way. And yet they followed him as their leader, though as one accursed. I saw that Cain was severely punished, but not damned.

One of Cain's descendants was Tubalcain, the originator of numerous arts, and the father of the giants. I have frequently

---

[1] Anne Catherine added that the city, or place of habitation, which she described in this way insofar as it occupied a specific locale (which during his life as an exile Cain dared not quit) was later divided into two again.

seen that, when the angels fell, a certain number had a moment of repentance and did not in consequence fall as low as the others. Later on these fallen spirits took up their abode on a high, desolate, and wholly inaccessible mountain whose site at the time of the deluge became a sea, the Black Sea, I think. They were permitted to exercise their evil influence upon men in proportion as the latter strayed further from God. After the deluge they disappeared from that region and were confined to the air. They will not be cast into hell before the Last Day.

I saw Cain's descendants becoming more and more godless and sensual, and how here, just as in paradise, satan always followed especially close behind the women. God said to the serpent, "You will prick the seed of woman in the heel."[1] They settled further and further up that mountain ridge where were the fallen spirits. Those spirits took possession of many of the women, ruled them completely, and taught them all sorts of seductive arts. Their children were very large. They possessed a quickness, an aptitude for everything, and they gave themselves up entirely to the wicked spirits as their instruments. And so arose on this mountain, and spread far around, a wicked race that by violence and seduction sought to entangle Seth's posterity likewise in their own corrupt ways. Then God declared to Noah his intention to send the deluge. During the building of the ark, Noah had to suffer terribly from those people.

I have seen many things connected with the race of giants. They could with ease carry enormous stones high up the mountain, they could accomplish the most stupendous feats. They could walk straight up trees and walls just as I have seen others possessed by the devil doing. They could effect the most wonderful things, they could do whatever they wished; but all was pure jugglery and delusion due to the agency of the demon. It is for that reason I have such a horror of every species of jugglery and fortune-telling. These people could form all kinds of images out

---

[1] An apparent reference to Gen. 3:15: "The Lord God said to the serpent, 'Because you have done this, I will put enmity between thee and the woman, and between thy seed and her seed: he shall bruise thy head, and thou shalt bruise his heel.'"

of stone and metal, but of the knowledge of God they had no longer a trace. They sought their gods in the creatures around them. I have seen them scratch up a stone, form it into an extravagant image, and then adore it. They worshipped also a frightful animal and all kinds of ignoble things. They knew all things, they could see all things, they were skilled in the preparing of poisons, they practiced sorcery and every species of wickedness. The women invented music. I saw them going around among the better tribes trying to seduce them to their own abominations. They had no dwelling houses, no cities, but they raised massive round towers of shining stone. Under those towers were little structures leading into great caverns wherein they carried on their horrible wickedness. From the roofs of these structures the surrounding country could be seen; and by mounting up into the towers and looking through tubes, one could see far into the distance. But it was not like looking through tubes made to bring distant objects into view. The power of the tubes to which I here allude was effected by satanic agency. They that looked through them could see where the other tribes were settled. Then they marched against them, overcame them, and lawlessly carried all before them. That same spirit of lawlessness they exercised everywhere. I saw them sacrificing children by burying them alive in the earth. God overthrew that mountain at the time of the deluge.[1] The towers of these godless people were made of shimmering stone or earth, angular at the bottom and not too tall, although always in the process of being raised higher.

---

[1] At this juncture in the notes we find the following remarks by Brentano: "Here we find traces of the myth of the Titans. Uranus joined with Gaia (earth), and their children (the Titans) were bound up in the earth (in Tartarus) after their birth. The Titans also were masters of (cunning) tricks. And if we consider the castration of Uranus (by Cronos, youngest and most ambitious of the Titans, set to this task by his mother Gaia) and the casting of his power of reproduction into the sea, we may see therein an image of the other form of procreation within Noah's ark; and that the birth of Venus (or Aphrodite) through this power represented a new point of entry for the enemy (the devil) to work into humankind and further develop a new and godless race. Ham also saw the genitals of his father (Noah) uncovered, wherewith commenced a new curse, a new depraved race, a new worship of the devil, new

ON Friday, September 30, AD 29, the shepherds Jesus was then visiting conducted him and the disciples in the direction of Bethlehem. They arrived at the dwellings of the sons of the three shepherds who had visited him at his birth. These three shepherds had in the meantime died. Their burial place was an isolated hill where there was a vineyard. After visiting their graves, Jesus and his followers, accompanied by some shepherds, visited the cave where he had been born. The sabbath was just beginning and the lamps had been lighted in the crib cave when the shepherds brought Jesus hither. The crib itself still occupied the same place. Jesus pointed out to the shepherds something that they did not know; that is, the exact spot upon which he was born. He gave them an instruction and they celebrated the sabbath in the cave. He told his hearers that his heavenly Father had chosen this place for his nativity at the time of Mary's immaculate conception, and I saw that it had been the theater of several significant events of the Old Testament. Abraham and Jacob had been within its walls, and before them had Seth, the Child of Promise, been born therein of Eve, after a penance of seven years. An angel appeared to Eve on that occasion, telling her that this was the Seed that God had given her in the place of Abel. Seth was for a long time hidden here and nursed, also in the suckling cave of Abraham's nurse Maraha; for, as Jacob's sons pursued Joseph, so did the brothers of Seth pursue him. The suckling cave was now Maraha's tomb.

On Saturday, July 22, AD 30, it was shown to me that Jesus

---

works and arts, Babylon, and schools of magic. The destruction of the tower of Babel was a new intervention by God, but we still find there the realm of the devil, Semiramis, and the whore of Babylon.

"And so that first evil (artificial) mountain, i.e., the building of the tower, Babylon, etc., represents the devil's adversarial architectural response to the City of God, the City on the Hill, the heavenly Jerusalem as against the terrestrial Jerusalem. This rush on the part of human beings toward the heights, to build higher and higher—could this not point to an elevated setting of paradise? Anne Catherine always saw Adam as staggering downward upon his fall. But on one occasion she said, 'paradise remains still in connection with the earth.'" CB chiefly prayed and sorrowed on the Mount of Olives because Adam and Eve when driven from paradise had here first trodden the inhospitable earth. I saw them in that cave sorrowing and praying, and it was on this mountain—which Cain was cultivating for the first time—that he became so enraged as to resolve to kill Abel. I thought of Judas. I saw Cain murdering his brother in the vicinity of Mount Golgotha, and on the Mount of Olives called by God to account for the same. Daybreak found Jesus back again in Bethany.

Enoch

I SAW Enoch and Noah, what they represented, what they effected; on the other side, I saw the ever-active empire of hell and the infinitely varied manifestations and effects of an earthly, carnal, diabolical idolatry.

Enoch, Noah's ancestor, opposed the wicked race of the giants by his teachings. He wrote much. He was a very good man and one very grateful to God. In many parts of the open fields he raised altars of stone, and there the fruits of the earth flourished. He gave thanks to God and offered sacrifice to Him. Chiefly in his family was religion preserved and handed down to Noah. Enoch was taken up to paradise. There he waits at the entrance gate, whence with another (Elijah) he will come again before the Last Day.[1]

Later Destiny Regarding Enoch

AFTER the deluge, when Tubal [see below] with his family separated from Noah, I saw among them that child of Mosoch, Hom,[2] who had gone with Tubal into the ark. Hom was taught by the devil in many ways, such as to oppose or vitiate the teachings of Enoch [as is described further below]. The father of Jam-

---

[1] Elsewhere Anne Catherine says: "I always see the place where Adam was created from the earth as a beautiful white mountain rising before the entrance to paradise, where Enoch and Elijah now lie."

[2] See "Hom" below.

shid[1] had been a pupil of Hom, and Hom left him his spirit in order that he might then be the one who would succeed him [as is also described later]. Jamshid spoke constantly of Enoch.

Of the Samanenses whom Melchizedek[2] settled in Palestine, I saw long before the coming of Abraham three men on the so-called bread mountain in the neighborhood of Tabor. They lived in caves. They were of a browner complexion than Abraham and were clothed in skins. They bound a great leaf on their head to protect them from the sun. Their life, modeled on that of Enoch, was a holy one. Their religion was simple though full of mysterious signification and they had visions and revelations which they easily interpreted. Their religion taught that God would unite himself with humankind and for that union they must prepare in every possible way.

At time of Joseph and Asenath,[3] when the Egyptian pagan priests intended to read the stars, they fasted as a preparation, performed certain purifications, clothed themselves in sackcloth, and sprinkled themselves with ashes. While they gazed upon the stars from their tower, sacrifices were offered. The pagans of those times had a confused knowledge of the religious mysteries of the true God that had been handed down from Seth, Enoch, Noah, and the patriarchs to the chosen people—therefore were there so many abominations in their idolatry. The devil made use of them, as later on of heresy, to weave the pure, unclouded, authentic revelations of God into a snare for humankind's destruction.

ON Tuesday, September 26, AD 30, for the feast of Atonement, Jesus taught in the synagogue regarding penance. He spoke against those who practiced only bodily purification and did not restrain those desires of the soul that were evil. I saw also during

---

[1] See "Jamshid" (sometimes spelled Djemschid).

[2] See "Melchizedek," where the Samanenses, in particular three associates of Melchizedek (of whom as far as yet determined we know nothing from other sources), are further described.

[3] See "Joseph and Asenath" in *Mysteries of the Old Testament.*

another reading in the Temple that Elijah, after his death, wrote a letter to King Jehoram. The Jews would not believe it. They explained it in this way: They said that Elisha, who brought the letter to Jehoram, had given it to him as a prophetical letter bequeathed to himself by Elijah. I began myself to think it very strange, when suddenly I was transported to the East and, in my journey, passed the mountain of the prophets, which I saw covered with ice and snow. It was crowned with towers, presenting perhaps the appearance it wore in the time of Jehoram. I went on then eastwardly to paradise and saw therein the beautiful, wonderful animals walking and gamboling around. There too were the glistening walls and, lying asleep on either side of the gate, Enoch and Elijah. Elijah was in spirit gazing upon all that was then going on in Palestine.

On Thursday, February 1, AD 31, Jesus continued the teaching on the bread of life on the road leading into Bethsaida, this time saying quite plainly that he was the bread of life (John 6:35–51). Some two thousand people were present. All his instructions were accompanied by full explanations and quotations from the *Law* and the *Prophets*. But most of the Jews would not comprehend them. They took all literally according to the common, human acceptation, and asked: "What meaneth these words, that we should eat him? And eternal life? Who then has eternal life, and who can eat of him? Enoch and Elijah have been taken away from the earth, and they say that they are not dead; nor does anyone know whither Malachi has gone, for no one knows of his death. But apart from these, all other men must die."

Jesus replied by asking them whether they knew where Enoch and Elijah were and where Malachi was. As for himself, this knowledge was not concealed from him. But did they know what Enoch believed, what Elijah and Malachi prophesied? And he explained several of their prophecies.

Noah and His Family: Shem, Ham, Japhet

I SAW Noah, a simple-hearted old man, clothed in a long white garment. He was walking about in an orchard and pruning the trees with a crooked bone knife. Suddenly a cloud hovered over him and in it was a human figure. Noah fell on his knees. I saw that he was, then and there, interiorly instructed upon God's design to destroy humankind and commanded to build an ark. I saw that Noah grew sad at the announcement and that he prayed for the punishment to be averted. He did not begin the work at once.

Again the Lord appeared to him, twice in succession, commanding him to begin the building, otherwise he should perish with the rest of humankind. At last I saw Noah removing with all his family to the country in which Zoroaster, the Shining Star, subsequently dwelt. Noah settled in a high, woody, solitary re gion where he and his numerous followers lived under tents. Here he raised an altar and offered sacrifice to the Lord. Neither Noah nor any of his family built permanent houses because they put faith in the prophecy of the deluge. But the godless nations around laid massive foundations, marked off courts, and erected all kinds of buildings designed to resist the inroads of time and the attacks of an enemy.

There were frightful deeds upon the earth in those days. Men delivered themselves up to all kinds of wickedness, even the most unnatural. They plundered one another and carried off whatever suited them best; they laid waste homes and fields, they kidnapped women and maidens. In proportion to their increase in numbers, was the wickedness of Noah's posterity. They even robbed and insulted Noah himself. They had not fallen into this state of base degradation from want of civilization. They were not wild and barbarous; rather, they lived commodiously and had well-ordered households—but they were deeply imbued with wickedness. They practiced the most shameful idolatry, everyone making his own god of whatever pleased him best. By diabolical arts, they sought to seduce Noah's immediate family.[1]

---

[1] Mosoch [or Meshech], the son of Japhet [or Japheth] and grandson of Noah, was thus corrupted after he had, while working in the field, taken from them a poisonous beverage which intoxicated him. It was not wine, but the juice of a plant they were accustomed to drink in small quantities during their work, and whose leaves and fruit they chewed. Mosoch became the father of a son, who was named Hom (see below).

It was long before the ark was completed, for Noah often discontinued it for years at a time. Three times did God warn him to proceed with it. Each time Noah would engage workmen, recommence, and again discontinue in the hope that God would relent. But at last the work was finished.

I saw that in the ark, as in the cross, there were four kinds of wood: palm, olive, cedar, and cypress. I saw the wood felled and hewed upon the spot, and Noah bearing it himself upon his shoulders to the place of building, just as Jesus afterward carried the wood of his cross. The spot chosen for the construction of the ark was a hill surrounded by a valley.

First the bottom was put in. The ark was rounded in the back and the keel, shaped like a trough, and smeared with pitch. It had two storeys supported on hollow posts that stood one above another. These posts were not round trunks of trees; they were in oval sections filled with a white pith that became fibrous toward the center. The trunk was knotty, or furrowed, and great leaves grew around it without branches.[1] I saw the workmen punching the pith out with a tool. All other trees were cut into thin planks.

When Noah had carried all the materials to the appointed spot and arranged them in order, the building was begun. The bottom was put in and pitched, the first row of posts raised, and the holes in which they stood filled up with pitch. Then came the second floor with another row of posts for the third floor, and then the roof. The spaces between the posts were filled in with brown and yellow laths placed crosswise, the holes and chinks being stuffed with a kind of wool found on certain trees and plants and a white moss that grows very abundantly around some trees. Then all was pitched inside and outside. The roof was rounded. The entrance between the two windows was in the center of one side, a little more than halfway up. In the middle of the roof likewise was a square opening. When the ark had been entirely covered with pitch, it shone like a mirror in the sun.

Noah went on working alone and for a long time at the different compartments for the animals, as all were to be separate. Two

---

[1] Probably a species of palm. CB

passages extended through the middle of the ark, and back in the oval part, concealed by hangings, stood a wooden altar, the table of which was semicircular. A little in the front of the altar was a pan of coals. This was their fire. Right and left were spaces partitioned off for sleeping apartments. All kinds of chests and utensils were carried into the ark, and numerous seeds, plants, and shrubs were put into earth around the walls, which were soon covered with verdure. I saw something like vines carried in, and on them large yellow grapes, the bunches as long as one's arm.

No words can express what Noah endured from the malice and ill will of the workmen during the whole time that the ark was building. They mocked him, they insulted him in every way, they called him a fool. He paid them well in cattle, but that did not prevent their reviling him. No one knew why he was building the ark, therefore did they ridicule him.

When all was finished, I saw Noah giving thanks to God, Who then appeared to him. He told him to take a reed pipe and call all the animals from the four corners of the globe.

The nearer the day of chastisement approached, the darker grew the heavens. Frightful anxiety took possession of the whole earth; the sun no longer showed his face, and the roar of the thunder was unceasingly heard. I saw Noah going a short distance north, south, east, and west, and blowing upon his reed pipe. The animals came flocking at the sound and entered the ark in order, two by two, male and female. They went in by a plank laid from the entrance to the ground. When all were safe inside, the plank also was hoisted in. The largest animals, white elephants and camels, went in first. They were restless as at the approach of a storm, and it took several days for them all to enter. The birds flew in through the skylight and perched under the roof on poles and in cages, while the waterfowl went into the bottom of the vessel. The land animals were in the middle storey. Of such as are slaughtered, there were seven couples.

The ark, lying there by itself on the top of the hill, shone with a bluish light. At a distance it looked as if it were descending from the clouds.

And now the time for the deluge drew nigh. Noah had already announced it to his family. He took with him into the ark Shem,

Ham, and Japhet,[1] with their wives and their children. There were in the ark grandsons from fifty to eighty years old with their children small and large. All that had labored at its construction and who were good and free from idolatry entered with Noah. There were over one hundred people in the ark, and they were necessary, to give daily food to the animals and to clean after them.

I must say, for I always see it so, that the children of Shem, Ham, and Japhet all went into the ark. There were many little boys and girls in it—in fact all of Noah's family that were good, as has been said. holy scripture mentions only three of Adam's children—Cain, Abel, and Seth—and yet I see many others among them, and I always see them in pairs, boys and girls. And so too, in 1 Peter 3:20, only eight souls are mentioned as saved in the ark—that is, the four ancestral couples by whom, after the deluge, the earth was to be peopled. I also saw Hom[2] in the ark. The child was fastened by a skin into a bark cradle formed like a trough. I saw many infants cradled in a similar way, floating on the waters of the deluge.

When the ark rose on the waters, when crowds of people upon the surrounding mountains and in the high trees were weeping and lamenting, when the waters were covered with the floating bodies of the drowned and with uprooted trees, Noah and his family were already safe inside. Before he and his wife, his three sons, and their wives entered the ark, he once more implored God's mercy. Then, when all had entered, Noah drew in the plank and made fast the door. He left outside near relatives and their

---

[1] Elsewhere Anne Catherine reports that in addition to his three sons (Shem, Ham, and Japhet) Noah had with other wives many more children, who were dispersed widely. But only those arising from a certain legitimate genealogical line were counted and named, and daughters seldom mentioned at all. Only the three sons with the proper pedigree went into the ark. On the matter of age, and fathering or bearing of children, she says further that the patriarchs sired children well into old age, but with younger maidens, as women in that time did not remain fertile as long as the men—although in the earliest times they too could conceive into their hundredth year, and retained their beauty to that advanced age as well.

[2] Great-grandson of Noah. See "Hom."

families, who, during the building of the ark, had separated from him.[1]

Then burst forth a fearful tempest. The lightnings played in fiery columns, the rains fell in torrents, and the hill upon which the ark stood soon became an island. The misery was great, so great that I trust it was the means of many a soul's salvation. I saw a devil, black and hideous, with pointed jaws and a long tail, going to and fro through the tempest and tempting men to despair. Toads and serpents sought a hiding place in the crevices of the ark. Flies and vermin I did not see—they came into existence later to torment men.

I saw Noah offering sacrifice in the ark upon an altar covered with red, over which was a white cloth. In an arched chest were preserved the bones of Adam. During prayer and sacrifice, Noah laid them on the altar. I saw on the altar likewise the chalice of the Last Supper which during the building of the ark had been brought to Noah by three figures in long white garments. They looked like the three figures who announced to Abraham the birth of a son. They came from a city that was destroyed at the time of the deluge. They addressed Noah as one whose fame had reached them, and told him that he should take with him into the ark a mysterious Something that they gave him, in order that it might escape the waters of the deluge. The mysterious Thing was that chalice. In it lay a grain of wheat, large as a sunflower seed, and a vine branch. Noah stuck both into a yellow apple and put it into the chalice. The chalice had no cover, for the branch was to grow out of it.[2]

I saw the ark driving over the waters and dead bodies floating around. It rested upon a high rocky peak of a mountain chain far to the east of Syria, and there it remained for a long time. I saw

---

[1] Elsewhere Anne Catherine says that Jamshid's great-grandfather (that is, Japhet) and grandfather Tubal were in the ark.

[2] "After the dispersion of men at the building of the tower of Babel I saw that chalice in the possession of one of Shem's descendants in the country of Semiramis. He was the ancestor of the Samanenses, who were established at Canaan by Melchizedek. Hither they took the chalice."

that land was already appearing. It looked like mud covered with a greenish mold.

Immediately after the deluge, fish and shellfish began to be eaten. Afterward, as people multiplied, they ate bread and birds. They planted gardens, and the soil was so fruitful that the wheat they sowed produced ears as large as those of maize. The root from which Hom received his name was also planted. Noah's tent stood on the spot where, at a later period, was that of Abraham. In the plain and in the surrounding country, Noah's sons had their tents.

I saw the cursing of Ham. But Shem and Japhet received from Noah on their knees the Blessing. It was delivered to them with ceremonies similar to those later used by Abraham when giving over the same Blessing to Isaac. I saw the curse pronounced by Noah upon Ham moving toward the latter like a black cloud and obscuring him. His skin lost its whiteness, he grew darker. His sin was the sin of sacrilege, the sin of one who would forcibly enter the Ark of the Covenant. I saw a most corrupt race descend from Ham and sink deeper and deeper into darkness. I see that the dark, idolatrous nations are the descendants of Ham. It would be impossible for me to say how I beheld the nations increasing and extending and in many different ways falling into darkness and corruption. But with all that, many luminous rays streamed forth from them and sought the light.

When Tubal, the son of Japhet, with his own children and those of his brother Mosoch, sought counsel of Noah as to the country to which they should migrate, they were fifteen families in number. Noah's children already extended far around, and the families of Tubal and Mosoch also dwelt at some distance from Noah. But when Noah's children began to quarrel and oppress one another, Tubal desired to remove still farther off. He wanted to have nothing to do with Ham's descendants, who were already thinking of building the tower of Babel. He and his family heeded not the invitation received later to engage in that undertaking, and it was declined also by the children of Shem. The children of Shem took no active part in the work. They dwelt in a level country where palm trees and similar choice fruit grow. They were however obliged to contribute something toward the building, for they did not dwell so far distant at that period as they did later.

Tubal with his troop of followers appeared before Noah's tent, asking for directions as to whither he should go. Noah then dwelt upon a mountain range between Libanus and the Caucasus. He wept when he saw Tubal and his followers, for he loved that race, because it was better, more God-fearing, than those of Japhet's other children, and also because Jamshid's great-grandfather was a friend of Enoch, having passed much time with him speaking about holy things. He pointed out a region toward the northeast, charged them to be faithful to the commands of God and to the offering of sacrifice,[1] and made them promise to guard the purity of their descent and not to intermingle with the descendants of Ham. He gave them girdles and breastpieces that he had had in the ark. The heads of the families were to wear them when engaged in divine service and performing marriage ceremonies, in order to guard against malediction and a depraved posterity.

The ceremonies Noah used when offering sacrifice reminded me of the holy sacrifice of the mass. There were alternating prayers and responses, and Noah moved from place to place at the altar and bowed reverently. He gave them likewise a leathern bag containing a vessel made of bark in which was an oval golden box enclosing three other smaller vessels. They also received from him the roots or bulbs of the Hom plant,[2] rolls of bark or skins upon which were written characters, and round wooden blocks upon which signs were engraved.

---

[1] Anne Catherine here made brief mention of a sacrifice of grain, which Brentano cites in his notes, followed by question marks.

2 In Brentano's notes we find another passage concerning this subject: "He gave them also a leathern sack within which was a container fashioned of bark. I do not know what it contained, or have perhaps forgotten—perhaps it was what was contained in the golden box mentioned before, which carried within an egg. As well, he passed on a mucilagenous plant, such as had been kept in the ark also. I did not see this plant in its true, natural size, but as I had seen it in the ark. It had three brown leaves one above another around the stem, and the upper part looked like the heads of asparagus. It seems to me that they grew out a bulb. They had a thickish stalk that provided a flour that

These people were of a bright, reddish-yellow complexion and very beautiful. They were clothed in skins and woolen garments girdled at the waist, the arms alone bare. The skins they wore were scarcely drawn from the animal when they were clapped, still bloody, on the limbs. They fitted so tightly that my first thought was: those people are hairy. Not so, however, for their own skin was smooth as satin. With the exception of various kinds of seed, they did not take much baggage with them, since they were departing for a high region toward the northeast. I saw no camels, but they had horses, asses, and animals with spreading horns like stags. I saw them, Tubal's followers, on a high mountain where they dwelt one above another in long, low huts like arbors. I saw them digging the ground, planting, and setting out trees in rows. The opposite side of the mountain was cold. Later on the whole region became much colder. In consequence of this change in the climate, one of the grandsons of Tubal, the ancestor Jamshid,[1] led them further toward the southwest. With a few exceptions, all who had seen Noah and had taken leave of him died in this place—that is, on the mountain to which Tubal had led them. They who followed Jamshid were all born on the same mountain. They took with them the few surviving old men who had known Noah, carrying them very carefully in litters.

When Tubal with his family separated from Noah, I saw among them that child of Mosoch, Hom, who had gone with Tubal into the ark. Hom was already grown, and later on I saw him very different from those around him. The evil inclinations inherited from his mother mingled in him with the pure hereditary teachings of Enoch and Noah, to which the children of Tubal clung. Hom, by his false visions and revelations, misinterpreted and

---

was cooked into a dough, which was then rolled out thin and baked. It is a breadfruit, which grows rampant for miles along the way, wherever it can thrive. This plant they held to be holy, and many beliefs were associated with it. For example, if one consumed it in a state of devotion, there would be no pangs of hunger for days thereafter. There was more, but I cannot recall it."

Brentano: "Was the name of the plant perhaps Hom, and the grandfather of Jamshid so called also?"

Anne Catherine: "I believe so, but it is not entirely clear to me."

[1] See "Jamshid."

changed the ancient truth. He studied and pondered, watched the stars, and had visions which, by satan's agency, showed him deformed images of truth. Through their resemblance to truth, his doctrine and idolatry became the mothers of heresy. Tubal was a good man. Hom's manner of acting and his teaching were very displeasing to Tubal, who was greatly grieved to see one of his sons, the father of Jamshid, attach himself to Hom. I heard Tubal complaining: "My children are not united. Would that I had not separated from Noah!"

On another occasion Anne Catherine reported many of these same themes, but ordered differently, in another context:

Many who had previously worked peaceably on the tower of Babel boasted of their skill and the great services they had rendered in the undertaking. They formed parties and laid claim to certain privileges. This occasioned contradictions, animosities, and rebellion. There were at first only two tribes among the disaffected, and these, it was resolved, should be put down; but soon it was discovered that disunion existed among all. They struggled among themselves, they slew one another, they could no longer make themselves understood by one another, and so at last they separated and scattered over the whole earth. I saw Shem's race going farther southward, where later on was Abraham's home.

The Semites [Shemites] were less numerous than the children of Ham and Japhet, and among them the family of Heber and the ancestors of Abraham studiously refrained from encouraging the enterprise. Upon Heber, who took no part in the work, God cast His eyes; and amid the general disorder and corruption, He set him and his posterity apart as a holy nation. God gave him also a new and holy language possessed by no other nation, that thereby his race should be cut off from communication with all others. This language was the pure Hebrew, or Chaldaic. The first tongue, the mother tongue spoken by Adam, Shem, and Noah, was different, and it is now extant only in isolated dialects. Its first pure offshoots are the Zend, the sacred tongue of India, and the language of the Bactrians. In those languages words may be found exactly similar to the Low German of my native place. The book that I see in modern Ctesiphon, on the Tigris, is written in that language [see "The Book of Ctesiphon"].

Heber was still living at the time of Semiramis. His grandfather Arphaxad[1] was the favorite son of Shem. His wisdom was prodigious, but was gradually given over to idolatry and magical arts. Many idolatrous practices derive from him, as also theurgical arts associated with amulets, seals, and sayings connected with star magic. The Magi derive their origin from him.

I also saw Abraham with Sarah in Egypt. He went thither in obedience to a command from God; first, on account of the famine, and secondly to take possession of a treasure that had been carried there by one of Sarah's relatives. The treasure consisted of triangular pieces of gold strung together to form a genealogical table of the children of Noah, and especially of Shem down to Abraham's own time.[2]

Hom

WHEN the child Hom was born, Mosoch begged his brother Tubal to take it, and thus hide his guilt. Tubal did so out of fraternal affection. The child, with the stalks and sprouts of a certain viscous root, was laid by his mother before Tubal's tent. She hoped thereby to acquire a right over his inheritance; but the deluge was already at hand, and so her plans were fruitless. Tubal took the boy and had him reared in his family without betraying his origin. And so it happened in this way that the child was taken into the ark.

Tubal called the boy Hom, the name of the root whose sprouts lay near him as the only sign. The child was not nourished with milk, but with the same root. If that plant is allowed to grow up

---

[1] Arphaxad—Arpachshad or Arphacsad—was one of the five sons of Shem, the eldest son of Noah, see Gen. 10:22, 24; 11:10–13; 1 Chron. 1:17–18.

[2] Elsewhere Ann Catherine says: "While the Blessed Mother on Golgotha was crying to God, a sudden and irresistible impulse took possession of Jonadab, drove him out of the Temple, and up to Mount Calvary. He indignantly felt in his soul the ignominy of Ham, who mocked at his father Noah intoxicated with wine, and like another Shem, he hurried to cover his Redeemer. The executioners who crucified Jesus were Hamites, that is, descendants of Ham."

straight, it will reach the height of a man; but when it creeps along the ground, it sends up shoots like the asparagus, hard with tender tops. It is used as food and as a substitute for milk. The root is bulbous, and from it rises a crown of a few brown leaves. Its stem is tolerably thick and the pith is used as meal, cooked like pap or spread in thin layers and baked. Wherever it thrives, it grows luxuriantly and covers leagues of ground. I saw it in the ark. As the time for the deluge approached, all those of Noah's family who were good, as has been said, were brought into the ark. And I saw Hom also among those in the ark [see above]. After the deluge, as people multiplied, they planted gardens, and the root named Hom was also planted.

Later, at the time when Tubal with his family moved away from Noah, Hom was already grown, and later on I saw him very different from those around him. He was of large stature like a giant, and of a very serious, peculiar turn of mind. He wore a long robe; he was like a priest. He used to go alone to the summit of the mountain and there spend night after night. He observed the stars and practiced magic. He was taught by the devil to arrange what he saw in vision into a science, a religion, and thereby he vitiated and counteracted the teaching of Enoch. As I has been said already, the evil inclinations inherited from his mother mingled in him with the pure hereditary teachings of Enoch and Noah, to which the children of Tubal clung. By his false visions and revelations Hom misinterpreted and changed the ancient truth. He studied, pondered, and watched the stars, and by satan's agency had visions that presented twisted images of truth. Through their resemblance to truth, his doctrine and idolatry became the mothers of heresy.

Now, as has been said, Tubal was a good man, and Hom's manner and teaching were displeasing to him. He was much grieved to see one of his sons, the father of Jamshid, attach himself to Hom. I heard again Tubal complaining: "My children are not united. Would that I had not separated from Noah!"

Hom conducted the waters of two springs from the higher part of the mountain down to the dwellings. These soon united into one stream which after a short course swelled into a broad torrent. I saw Jamshid and his followers crossing it at their departure.

Hom received almost divine homage from his followers. He taught them that God exists in fire. He had also much to do with water and with that viscous root from which he derived his name. He planted it and solemnly distributed it as a sacred medicine and nourishment. This distribution at last became a ceremony of religion. He carried its juice or pap around with him in a brown vessel like a mortar. The axes were of the same material. They got them from people of another tribe that lived far away in a mountainous country and forged such implements by means of fire. I saw them on a mountain from which fire burst forth, sometimes in one place, sometimes in another. I think the vessel Hom carried around with him was made out of the melted metal or rock that flowed from the mountain, and which was caught in a mold.

Hom never married nor did he live to be very old. He published many of his visions referring to his own death. He himself put faith in them as did also Derketo and his other followers at a later period. But I saw him dying a frightful death, and the evil one carried him off body and soul; nothing remained of him. For that reason his followers thought that, like Enoch, he had been taken up to a holy dwelling place. The father of Jamshid had been a pupil of Hom, and Hom left him his spirit in order that he might then be the one who would succeed him.

Jamshid

ON account of his knowledge, Jamshid became the leader of his people. They soon became a nation, and were led by Jamshid still further south. Jamshid was very distinguished; he was well-educated and had embraced Hom's teachings. He was unspeakably lively and vigorous, much more active, and better also than Hom, who was of a dark, rigid disposition. He practiced the religion formulated by Hom, added many things of his own thereto, and gave much attention to the stars. His followers regarded fire as sacred. They were all distinguished by a certain sign that denoted their race. People at that time kept together in tribes; they did not intermingle then as now. Jamshid's special aim was to improve the races and maintain them in their original purity; he separated and transplanted them as seemed best to him. He left them perfectly free, and yet they were very submissive to him.[1]

On his marches Jamshid laid the foundations of tent cities, marked off fields, made long roads of stone, and formed settlements here and there of certain numbers of men and women, to whom he gave animals, trees, and plants. He rode around large tracks of land, striking into the earth with an instrument that he always carried in his hand, and his people then set to work in those places, grubbing and hacking, making hedges and digging ditches.

Jamshid was remarkably strict and just. I saw him as a tall old man, very thin and of a yellowish-red complexion. He rode a surprisingly nimble little animal with slender legs and black and yellow stripes, very much like an ass.

Jamshid rode around a tract of land just as our poor people go around a field on the heath by night, and thus appropriated it for cultivation. He paused here and there, plunged his grubbing axe into the ground or drove in a stake to mark the sites of future settlements. The instrument, which was afterward called Jamshid's golden plowshare, was in form like a Latin cross. It was about the length of one's arm and when drawn out formed with the shaft a right angle. With this instrument Jamshid made fissures in the earth. A representation of the same appeared on the side of his robe where pockets generally are. It reminded me of the symbol of office that Joseph and Asenath always carried in Egypt and with which they also surveyed the land, though that of Jamshid was more like a cross. On the upper part was a ring into which it could be run.

Jamshid wore a mantle that fell backward from the front. From his girdle to the knee hung four leathern flaps, two behind and two before, strapped at the side and fastened under the knee. His feet were bound with leather and straps. He wore a golden shield

[1] "The descendants of those races whom I now see wild and barbarous in distant lands and islands are not to be compared with their progenitors in point of personal beauty or manly character; for those early nations were noble and simple, yet withal most valiant. The races of the present day are also far less skillful and clever, and possess less bodily strength."

on his breast, which in the region of the ribs was cut through so as to conform to the individual ribs (most probably to make the whole more flexible). He had several similar breastplates to suit various solemnities. His crown was a pointed circlet of gold. The point in front was higher and bent like a little horn, and on the end of it waved something like a little flag.

Jamshid constantly spoke of Enoch. He knew that he had been taken away from the earth without undergoing death. He taught that Enoch had delivered over to Noah all goodness and all truth, had appointed him the father and guardian of all blessings, and that from Noah all these blessings had passed over to himself. He wore about him a golden, egg-shaped vessel in which, as he said, was contained something precious that had been preserved by Noah in the ark, and that had been handed down to himself. Wherever he pitched his tent, there the golden vessel was placed on a column, and over it, on elegant posts carved with all kinds of figures, a covering was stretched. It looked like a little temple. The cover of the vessel was a crown of filigree work. When Jamshid lighted fire, he threw into it something that he took out of the vessel. The vessel had indeed been used in the ark, for Noah had preserved the fire in it; but it was now the treasured idol of Jamshid and his people. When it was set up, fire burned before it, to which prayers were offered and animals sacrificed, for Jamshid taught that the Great God dwells in light and fire, and that he has many inferior gods and angels serving him.

All submitted to Jamshid. He established colonies of men and women here and there, gave them herds and permitted them to plant and build. They were not allowed to follow their own pleasure in the matter of marriage, for Jamshid treated them like cattle, assigning wives to his followers in accordance with his own views. He himself had several. One was very beautiful and of a better family than the others. Jamshid destined his son by her to be his successor.

By his orders great round towers or mounds were built, which were ascended by steps for the purpose of observing the stars. The women lived apart and in subjection. They wore short garments, the bodice and breast of material like leather, and some kind of stuff hung behind. Around the neck and over the shoulders they wore a full, circular cloak, which fell below the knee. On the shoulders and breast it was ornamented with signs or letters. From every country that he settled Jamshid caused straight roads to be made in the direction of Babel.

Jamshid always led his people to uninhabited regions where there were no nations to expel. He marched everywhere with perfect freedom, for he was only a founder, a settler. His race was of a bright reddish-yellow complexion like ochre, with fox-red hair— very handsome people. All were marked in order to distinguish the pure from those of mixed descent.

Jamshid marched over a high mountain covered with ice. I do not remember how he succeeded in crossing, but many of his followers perished. They had horses or asses; Jamshid rode on a little striped animal. A change of climate had driven them from their country. It became too cold for them, but it is warmer there now.

Occasionally he met on his march a helpless tribe either escaping from the tyranny of their chief or awaiting in distress the advent of some leader. They willingly submitted to Jamshid, for he was gentle, and he brought them grain and blessings. They were destitute exiles who, like Job, had been plundered and banished. I saw some poor people who had no fire and who were obliged to bake their bread on hot stones in the sun. When Jamshid gave them fire, they looked upon him as a god. He fell in with another tribe that sacrificed children who were deformed or who did not reach their standard of beauty. The little ones were buried up to the waist and a fire kindled around them. Jamshid abolished this custom. He delivered many poor children, whom he placed in a tent and confided to the care of some women. He afterward made use of them here and there as servants. He was very careful to keep the genealogical line pure.

Jamshid first marched in a southwesterly direction, keeping the prophet mountain to the south on his left; then he turned to the south, the mountain still on his left, but to the east. I think he afterward crossed the Caucasus. At that period, when those regions were swarming with human beings, when all was life and activity, our countries were but forests, wildernesses, and marshes; only off toward the east might be met a small, wandering tribe.

The Shining Star (that is, Zoroaster), who lived long after, was descended from Jamshid's son, whose teachings he revived. Jamshid wrote all kinds of laws on bark and tablets of stone. One long letter often stood for a whole sentence. Their language was as yet the primitive one, to which ours still bears some resemblance. Jamshid lived just prior to Derketo and her daughter, the mother of Semiramis.[1] He did not go to Babel himself, though his career ran in that direction.

I saw the history of Hom and Jamshid also as Jesus spoke of it before the pagan philosophers at Lanifa in the Isle of Cyprus [on Friday, May 11, AD 31]. These philosophers had in Jesus's presence spoken of Jamshid as the most ancient of the wise kings who had come from far beyond India. With a golden dagger received from God, he had divided off and peopled many lands, and had scattered blessings everywhere.

They questioned Jesus about him and the various wonders related to him. Jesus responded to their questions by saying that Jamshid was by nature a prudent man, a man wise according to flesh and blood; that he had been a leader of the nations; that upon the dispersion of men at the building of the tower of Babel he had led one race and settled countries according to a certain order; that there had been other leaders of that kind who had, indeed, led a worse life than he, because his race had not fallen into so great ignorance as many others.

But Jesus showed them also what fables had been written about Jamshid and that he was a false side picture, a counterfeit type, of the priest and king Melchizedek. He told them to notice the difference between Jamshid's race and that of Abraham. As the stream of nations moved along, God had sent Melchizedek to the best families to lead and unite them, to prepare for them lands and abiding places in order that they might preserve themselves unsullied, and in proportion to their degree of worthiness be found more or less fit to receive the grace of the Promise. Who Melchizedek was, Jesus left to themselves to determine; but of one thing they might be certain, he was an ancient type of the future but then fast approaching fulfillment of the Promise. The

[1] Elsewhere Anne Catherine says that Jamshid met the mother of Semiramis.

sacrifice of bread and wine that he had offered would be fulfilled and perfected, and would continue till the end of time.

Jesus's words upon Jamshid and Melchizedek were so clear, so indisputable, that the philosophers exclaimed in astonishment: "Master, how wise thou art! It would almost seem as if thou didst live in that time, as if thou didst know all these people even better than they knew themselves!" Jesus said to them many more things concerning the prophets, both the greater and the minor, and he dwelt especially upon Malachi.

The Tower of Babel

THE building of the tower of Babel was the work of pride. The builders aimed at constructing something according to their own ideas, and thus resisted the guidance of God. When the children of Noah had become very numerous, the proudest and most experienced among them met to resolve upon the execution of some work so great and so strong as to be the wonder of all ages to come and cause the builders to be spoken of as the most skillful, the most powerful of men. They thought not of God, but sought their own glory only. Had it been otherwise—as I was distinctly told—God would have allowed their undertaking to succeed. As has been said before, the children of Shem took no active part in the work.

The tower of Babel was built upon rising ground, about two leagues in circumference, around which lay an extensive plain covered with fields, gardens, and trees. To the foundations of the tower, that is up to its first storey, twenty-five very broad, stone walks—for men and beasts of burden—led from all sides of the plain. Twenty-five tribes were engaged in the building, and each tribe had its own road to the tower. Off in the distance where these roads began each tribe had its own particular city that, in time of danger or attack, they might flee to the tower for shelter. The tower was intended likewise to serve as a temple for their idolatrous worship. The stone roads were, where they took their rise in the plain, tolerably far apart; but around the tower they lay so close that the intervening spaces were not greater than the breadth of a wide street. Before reaching the tower, they were connected by cross arches, and between every two there opened a gateway about ten feet wide into its base. When these gently inclined roads had reached a certain height they were pierced by single arcades. Near the tower the arcades were double, one above the other, so that through them one could make the circuit of the building, even around the lowest part, under all the roads. Above the arches that connected the inclined roads were walks, or streets, running horizontally around the tower. Those gently rising roads extended like the roots of a tree. They were designed in part as supporting counter-pillars to strengthen the foundation of the immense building and partly as roads for the conveyance, from all points, of building materials and other loads to the first storey of the tower.

Between these extended bases were encampments upon sub-structures of stone. In many places the tops of the tents rose above the roads that ran through them. From every encampment steps cut in the walls led up to the walks. One could go all around the tower through the encampments and arches and under the stone roads.

The inclined stone streets, each the width of a broad thorough-fare, lay about a quarter of an hour removed from each other at their outer perimeter.[1] Where they intersected the tower, the distance between the roadways was reduced to approximately the same as their own width, so that the circumference of the tower itself, by this count, was about fifty times that width. Along the gently rising streets were many level areas generally crossed in turn by series of arches leading to the next ring around the tower, and cutting also through the encampment of tents. In truth, these roadways were broader than a thoroughfare if one took into account the smaller pathways and flights of stairs branching off from them into the tent city.

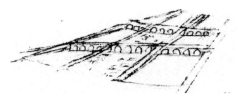

Besides the occupants of the encampments there were others who lived in the vaults and spaces on either side of and under the stone roads. In and around the whole building swarmed innumerable living beings. It was like a huge anthill. Countless elephants, asses, and camels toiled up and down the roads with their heavy burdens. Although these burdens were far broader than the animals themselves, yet several could with ease pass one another on the roads. On them were halting places for feeding and unloading

---

[1] Reckoning twenty-five quarter-hours, together with the breadth of the thoroughfares times twenty-five, we arrive at the figure of six hours as representing the circumference of the circle at the point where the roads commenced.

the animals, also tents on the level spaces and even factories. I saw animals without a guide bearing their burdens up and down.

The gateways in the basement of the tower led into a labyrinth of halls, passages, and chambers. From this lower part of the tower one could mount by steps cut out on all sides. A spiral[1] walk wound from the first storey around the exterior of the poly-gonal building. The interior at this point consisted of cellars, immense and secure, covered chambers and passages.

The building was begun on all sides at once, and all tended to one central point where at first stood a large tent encampment. They used tiles, also immense hewn stones, which they hauled to the site. The surface of the walks was quite white and glistened in the sun. At a distance the sight it presented was wonderful. The tower was planned most skillfully. I was told that it would have been finished—and would yet be standing as a magnificent monument of human skill—had it been erected to the honor of God. But the builders thought not of God. Their work was the offspring of presumption.

The names of those who had contributed to the grandeur and magnificence of the building were inscribed with words of praise in the vaults and on the pillars; in the former by means of different colored stones and on the latter in large characters. There were no kings, but only the heads of the different families, and they ruled according to common counsel.

The stones employed in the building were skillfully wrought. They fitted into one another, held one another together. There were no raised figures on the building but many parts of it were inlaid with colored stones, and here and there were figures hewn in niches. Canals and cisterns were constructed for water supplies. All lent a helping hand. Even the women trod the clay with their feet. The men worked with breast and arms bare, the most distinguished wearing a little cap with a button. Even in very early times women kept the head covered.

The building so increased in bulk and height that on account of the shade it cast it was quite cold on one side, while on the other the reflection of the sun's rays made it very hot. For thirty years

---

[1] "Snail-shaped" is the literal expression found in the notes.

the work went on. They were at the second storey. They had already encircled and walled in the interior with towerlike columns, had already recorded their names and races thereon in colored stones—when the confusion broke forth.

I saw one sent by God, Melchizedek, going around among the leaders and the masters of the building. He called upon them to account for their conduct and he announced to them the chastisement of God. And now began the confusion. Many who had up to this time worked on peaceably now boasted of their skill and the great services they had rendered in the undertaking. They formed parties, they laid claim to certain privileges. This occasioned contradictions, animosities, and rebellion.

There were at first only two tribes among the disaffected, and these—it was resolved—should be put down; but soon it was discovered that disunion existed among all. They struggled among themselves, slew one another, could no longer make themselves understood by one another. And so at last they separated and scattered over the whole earth. I saw Shem's race going farther southward, where later on was Abraham's home.

I saw one of Shem's race. He was a good man but did not follow his leader. On account of his wife he preferred staying among the wicked ones of Babel. He became the leader of the Samanenses, a race that always held themselves aloof from others. Under the cruel Semiramis, Melchizedek transplanted them to Palestine.[1]

When in my childhood I had the vision of the building of the tower, I used to reject it because I could not understand it. I had,

---

[1] On another occasion, as reported above (here abbreviated) in connection with Noah, Anne Catherine said: "I saw on the altar of Noah the chalice of the Last Supper which during the building of the ark had been brought to Noah by three figures in long white garments. They looked like the three men that announced to Abraham the birth of a son. They told him that he should take with him into the ark a mysterious Something that they gave him, in order that it might escape the waters of the deluge. The mysterious Thing was that chalice. After the dispersion of men at the building of the tower of Babel, I saw that chalice in the possession of one of Shem's descendants in the country of Semiramis. He was the ancestor of the Samanenses, who were established at Canaan by Melchizedek. Hither they took the chalice." See "Melchizedek and the Three Samanenses."

of course, seen nothing like it, no buildings but our farmhouses whence the cows go out by the fireplace, and the city of Coesfeld. More than once I thought it must be heaven. But I had the vision again and again, and always in the same way I see it still, and I have also seen how it looked in Job's time.

ON Monday, August 28, AD 30, Jesus and the disciples arrived around two o'clock in the afternoon at Abel-Mehola. Here he healed many sick people. This was frowned upon by the disapproving Pharisees. Then he was taken to a small schoolhouse that had been in existence even in the time of Rebecca and Jacob. I saw that they studied here in Rebecca's time the religion of Abraham, learning among many other things all about the deluge, about Noah's escape in the ark, about Shem, Ham, and Japhet, about Ham's sin and the reiterated wickedness of men at the tower of Babel. They were told of the building of that tower, of its destruction, of the confusion of tongues, and of the dispersion of men now become enemies to one another. Necromancy and idolatry were practiced likewise at the tower of Babel.

Six weeks later, on Friday, October 13, AD 30, Jesus and the disciples traveled to Aruma. In the synagogue Jesus taught of Abraham's vocation and his journey to Egypt, of the Hebrew tongue, of Noah, Heber, Peleg, and Job. The lessons were from Genesis 12 and Isaiah. Jesus said that Heber, like Adam, Seth, and Noah, had spoken that first mother tongue. But at the building of the tower of Babel this had been confused and broken up into numerous dialects. In order to separate Heber entirely from the rest of men, God had given him a language of his own, the holy, ancient Hebrew, without which he and his descendants would never have been able to keep themselves pure and a distinct race. Before that, as has been said, Heber, like Adam, Seth, and Noah, had spoken that first mother tongue, which at the building of the tower of Babel had been confused and broken up into dialects.

During the following spring, on Friday, May 11, AD 31, Jesus and the disciples took a walk with seven [formerly pagan] philosophers who had received baptism. The philosophers made mention of one of the most ancient of the wise kings who had come from the mountainous regions beyond India. He was called Jamshid. With a golden dagger received from God he had divided off many lands, peopled them, and shed blessing everywhere. They asked Jesus about him and the many wonders which they related of him. Jesus answered that Jamshid, who had been a leader of the people, was a man naturally wise and intelligent in the things of sense. Upon the dispersion of men at the time of the building of the tower of Babel he had put himself at the head of a tribe and taken possession of lands according to certain regulations. He had fallen less deeply into evil, because the race to which he belonged was itself less corrupt.

Nimrod

ONE of the chief leaders in the tower building was Nimrod. He was actually named Belus and afterward honored as a deity under that name. He was the founder of the race that honored Derketo and Semiramis as goddesses.[1] He built Babylon mostly from the stones of the tower, and Semiramis greatly embellished it. He also laid the foundation of Nineveh and built substructures of stones for tent dwellings.

He was a great hunter in the face of the Lord, which means he was hunter and tyrant. At that period savage animals were very numerous and they committed fearful ravages. The hunting expeditions fitted out against them were as grand as military expeditions. They who slew these wild animals were honored as gods.

Nimrod also drove men together and subdued them. He practiced idolatry, he was full of cruelty and witchcraft. He was powerful and virile, having many children with many woman—a great many children, one of them being the mother of Semiramis, to whose pagan idolatry Semiramis was much devoted.

If I recollect correctly, Nimrod lived to be two hundred and seventy years old. He was of sallow complexion, and from early youth he had led a wild life. He was an instrument of the powers of evil. He was much given to star worship. Of the numerous fig-

---

[1] Below, Anne Catherine says Nimrod was the father of the mother of Semiramis.

ures and pictures that he traced in the planets and constellations, and according to which he prophesied concerning the different nations and countries, he sought to reproduce representations, which he set up as gods. The Egyptians owe their sphinx to him, of which he had a vision on behalf of this nation and land, as also their many-armed and many-headed idols. For seventy years, Nimrod busied himself with the histories of these idols, with ceremonial details relative to their worship and the sacrifices to be offered them, also with the forming of the pagan priesthood.

By his diabolical wisdom he had subjected the races he led to the building of the tower, who at that time still spoke one language. When the confusion of tongues arose, many of those tribes broke away from him, the wildest of which went to Egypt and Africa.[1] Nimrod built Babylon, subjected the country around, and laid the foundation of the Babylonian Empire. Among his numerous children were Ninus and Derketo. The last-mentioned was honored as a goddess.

Derketo

FROM Derketo to Semiramis I saw three generations of daughters. Derketo was a tall, powerful woman. I saw her clothed in skins with numerous straps and animals' tails hanging about her. Her head was covered by a cap made of the feathers of birds. I saw her with a great train of followers, male and female, sallying forth from the neighborhood of Babylon. She was constantly in vision, engaged in prophesying, offering sacrifice, founding cities, or roving about. She and her followers drove before them scattered tribes with their herds, prophesied on the subject of good dwelling places, piled up stones, some of which were immense, offered sacrifice, and practiced all kinds of wickedness. She drew all to herself. She was sometimes here, sometimes there. She was everywhere honored. She had in her old age a daughter who played a part similar to her own.

I saw this vision in a plain, by which was signified the origin of

---

[1] Elsewhere we read that the wildest of these tribes followed Mizraim to Egypt.

the abomination. Lastly, I saw Derketo as a frightful old woman in a city by the sea. She was again carrying on her sorcery by the seashore. She was in a state of diabolical ecstasy, and she was proclaiming to her people that she must die for them, give her life for them. She told them that she could remain with them no longer, but that she would be transformed into a fish, and as such be always near them. She gave directions for the worship to be paid her, and in presence of the assembled multitude plunged into the sea. Soon after, a fish arose above the waves and the people saluted it with sacrifices and abominations of all kinds. Their divinations were full of mysteries, signs, etc., connected with water. Through Derketo's instrumentality an entire system of idolatry arose.

After Derketo, I saw another woman, the daughter of Derketo. She appeared to me on a low mountain, which signified that her position was more powerful than that of her mother. This was still in Nimrod's time, for they belonged to the same age. I saw this daughter leading a life even wilder and more violent than her mother's had been. She was engaged most of her time in hunting, attended by crowds of followers. She often went to a distance of three hundred miles, pursued wild animals, offered sacrifice, practiced witchcraft, and prophesied. In this way numerous places were founded and idolatrous worship established. I saw this woman fall into the sea while struggling with a hippopotamus.[1]

In the earliest times, power over others was held more peaceably and was vested in many; later on, unlimited jurisdiction was possessed by single individuals. These latter then became the leaders, the gods of their followers, and they formulated various systems of idolatrous worship, each according to his or her own ideas. They could also perform wonders of skill, valor, and invention, for they were full of the spirit of darkness. Thence arose whole tribes, first rulers and priests combined, later of priests alone. I have seen that in those days women of this stamp were

---

[1] "At that time I saw her daughter Semiramis upon a lofty mountain surrounded by all the kingdoms and treasures of the world, as if satan were showing them to her, giving them to her. I saw that Semiramis put the finishing touch to every abomination of the Babylonian race."

more numerous than men. They were all in interior communication, connected with one another by feelings, thoughts, and influence. Many things narrated of them are imperfect recitals of their ecstatic, or mesmeric expressions relative to themselves, their origin, their doings uttered sometimes by themselves, at other times by their devilish clairvoyants.[1]

Water was held specially sacred by those early idolaters. It entered into all their service. Whether divinations or ecstasies, they always began by gazing into water. They had ponds consecrated to that purpose. After some time their ecstatic state became habitual, and even without the aid of water they had their evil visions. I have seen the way in which they had those visions and it was indeed singular. The whole earth, with all that it contains, seemed to be once more under water, but veiled as in a dark sphere. Tree stood under tree, mountain under mountain, water under water. I saw that those enchantresses beheld all that was going on: wars, nations, perils, and so forth, just as is done at the present day—only with this difference, that the former put what they saw into effect, made good what they saw. Here was a nation to be subdued, here one to be taken by surprise, there a city to be built. Here were famous men and women, and there was the plan by which they might be outwitted; in fine, every item of their diabolical worship was seen before reduced to practice by those females. Derketo saw in vision that she should cast herself into the sea and be transformed into a fish, and what she saw, she hesitated not to carry into effect. Even the abominations practiced in their worship were all mirrored in the water before they put them into execution.

In the age in which Derketo's daughter lived, dykes and roads began to be constructed. She raided down into Egypt itself. Her

---

[1] "The Jews also had many secret arts in Egypt. But Moses, the seer of God, rooted them out. Among the rabbis, however, many such things existed as points of learning. Later on these secret arts became low, vulgar practices among wandering tribes, and they still exist in witchcraft and superstition. But they have all sprung from the same tree of corruption, from the same low kingdom of darkness. I see the visions of all that engage in such practices either just above or entirely under the earth. There is an element of the same in magnetism."

whole life was one series of moving and hunting expeditions. Her adherents belonged to the tribe that had plundered Job in Arabia. The diabolical worship of Derketo's people became systematized first in Egypt. Here it took such hold that, while the witches sat in the temples and in chambers on strange-looking seats before various kinds of mirrors, their visions, communicated while actually seen, were reported by the priests to hundreds of men who engraved them upon the stone walls of caverns.

Strange that I should see all those abominable chief instruments of darkness always in unconscious communion with one another! I saw similar actions and things going on in different places among similar instruments of the evil one. The only difference among them was that which arose from the diversity of manners and customs among the several nations and the different degrees of depravity into which they had fallen. Some had not as yet sunk so deep in these abominations and were not so far removed from the truth—those for instance from whom the family of Abraham and the races of Job and the three kings sprang, as also the star worshippers of Chaldea and they that had the Shining Star (Zoroaster).[1]

Derketo, her daughter, and her granddaughter Semiramis lived to be very old, according to the general age of that time. They were tall, powerful, mighty, such as would almost frighten us in our day. They were inconceivably bold, fierce, shameless, and they carried out with astonishing assurance whatever the evil one had shown them in vision. They felt their own power, they thought themselves divinities; they were facsimiles of those furious sorcerers on the high mountain that perished in the deluge.

It is touching to see how the holy patriarchs, although they had frequent revelations from God, had nevertheless to suffer and to struggle unremittingly in order to keep clear of the abominations that surrounded them. And again, it is affecting to remember in what secret, what painful, ways salvation at last came upon earth,

---

[1] "When Jesus Christ came upon earth, when the earth was soaked with his blood, the fierce influence of such practices was considerably diminished, and witchcraft lost much of its power. Moses was a seer from his cradle, but he was according to God, and he always practiced what he saw."

while all went well with demonolatry, while all things were made to subserve its interests.

When I saw all this, the immense influence exercised by those goddesses and the high worship they received over all the earth; and, on the other side, when I contemplated Mary's little band with whose symbolical picture in the cloud of Elijah the philosophers of Cyprus sought to couple their lying abominations; when I saw Jesus, the fulfillment of all promises, poor and patient, standing before them teaching and afterward going to meet his cross—ah, that made me inexpressibly sad! But after all, this is the history of the truth and the light ever shining in the darkness, and the darkness not comprehending it. And so it has been and so it is still, the same old story even down to our own day.

But the mercy of God is infinite. I have seen that at the time of the deluge, many, very many, were saved from eternal punishment. Fright and anguish converted them to God. They went to purgatory, and Jesus freed them on his descent into hell.

Semiramis

THE mother of Semiramis was born in the region of Nineveh. Outwardly noble and demure, she was also, as has already been said, much embroiled in idolatry and magic, and an uncommonly accomplished huntress. She was held in such high regard that it was said she would bear a divine child. The father of Semiramis was a native of Syria, a handsome man, with whom her mother was quite infatuated. He also was sunk in the most detestable idolatry. He was put to death after the child's birth, his murder being in some way connected with, or in consequence of, their divinations.[1]

---

[1] "Among these tribes that descended from the patriarchs through sidelines there were all kinds of obscure concepts, stories, and devilish visions of the seed of the woman who would step upon the head of the serpent—in which connection they mixed all kinds of lewdness into their religious practices, human sacrifices, and the most horrible things. Based on dreams and star prophecies, the idolatrous priests performed atrocious sacrifices accompanied by magic and prayers. The looked to the stars, consulted oracles, and placed

Semiramis was born far away at Ascalon, in Palestine, and then taken by pagan priests to some shepherds in a wilderness. She spent much of her time during her childhood alone on a mountain. I saw her mother and the pagan priests turning aside when on their hunting expeditions to visit her. I saw too the devil under various forms playing with her, like John in the desert going around with angels. I saw near her birds of brilliant plumage who brought to her all sorts of exotic foods. I do not remember all that went on connected with her, but it was the most horrible idolatry. She was beautiful, full of intelligence and seductive arts, and everything succeeded with her.

In obedience to certain divinations she became the wife of one of the chief shepherds of the king of Babylon, and later on she married the king himself. This king had conquered a nation further to the east, and had dragged a part of them to his own country as slaves. Some time after, when Semiramis reigned alone, many of them were oppressed by her and forced to labor at her extravagant buildings. Semiramis was looked upon as a goddess by her nation.

The hunting expeditions carried on by Semiramis's mother were wilder than those she herself conducted. She, the mother, went about with a little army mounted on camels, striped asses, and horses. Once I saw them in Arabia toward the Red Sea on a great hunt at the time when Job dwelt in his city there. The huntresses were very dexterous and they sat on horseback like men. They were fully clothed to the knee, below which the limbs were laced with straps. On the feet they wore soles with two high heels, upon which were colored figures. They wore short, closely fitting jackets made of fine feathers of the most diverse hues and pat-

---

horrible idols in front of the fornicators. They conjured the gods through songs and prayer, hoping thus that the child conceived [in these rituals] might acquire the desired, great qualities. This was all a mimicry of the true, veiled promise of the coming of the Restorer and Redeemer, and his holy conception. From the time of Adam, a religious mystery was connected with reproduction. Certain children were the elect—they received the Blessing, the transmission of the Mystery. The less noble lines of descent, which in many ways fell into idolatry and magic, came to the most evil horror. All religious service should, however, be centered in holy procreation."

terns. Crossed over the arms and breast were straps trimmed with feathers. The shoulders were covered with a cape, likewise of feathers, and set with glittering stones and pearls. On the head they wore a kind of hat of red silk or wool. Over the face fell a veil in two halves, either of which could be used as a protection from wind and dust. A short mantle completed their costume.

Their hunting weapons consisted of spears, bows, and arrows; at their side hung a shield. The savage animals had multiplied astonishingly. The hunters drove them together from all parts of immense districts and slew them. They also dug pits and covered them as snares. When the beasts fell into them, they were soon dispatched with hatchets and clubs.

At this time the raiment of less important women covered only their midriff, leaving the upper body naked, but for individual straps worn not unlike the suspenders of men of our own time. Women of a somewhat higher station might wear a thin shirt underneath, and perhaps also a cloth covering like a shroud.

I saw the mother of Semiramis hunting the animal described by Job under the name of behemoth, also swine-like animals with colored spots, tigers, lions, and many others. I saw no monkeys in those early times. I saw similar hunts upon the water, upon which idolatry and numerous abominations were generally practiced.

The mother was outwardly not so dissolute as Semiramis but she possessed a diabolical nature with amazing strength and temerity. What a frightful thing, to plunge into the sea in her struggle with such a monster as a hippopotamus! Mounted on a creature with two humps (a dromedary), she pursued the animal until dromedary and rider plunged into the waves.[1]

Semiramis, returning home from Africa after one of her hunting or military expeditions, went to Egypt. This kingdom had been founded by Mizraim (a son of Ham) some time after the confusion of tongues consequent upon the destruction of the tower of Babel. When he came there he had found already several

---

[1] Regarding this episode Anne Catherine says elsewhere: "The mother later met her end when passing through water mounted upon a camel, though I do not recall the particulars. Thereafter she was worshipped as a goddess of the chase and benefactress of humankind."

scattered tribes of degenerate neighboring races. Egypt was peopled by several races, and ruled sometimes by one, sometimes by another. When Semiramis went to Egypt, four cities were in existence. The oldest was Thebes, where a lighter, more slender and agile race lived than in the city of Memphis, whose inhabitants were short and thickset. Memphis lay upon the left bank of the Nile, over which was a long bridge. On the right bank was the place where, in Moses's time, Pharaoh's daughter lived. The darker inhabitants with woolly hair were even in those first ages slaves, and they had never ruled in Egypt. They that first went thither and built Thebes came, I think, from Africa; the others from over the Red Sea and from where the Israelites entered. A third city was called Chume, later Hermopolis. It lies toward the north below Thebes.

Here Semiramis built a most singular tower, or pyramid—the other pyramids did not yet exist—of which no trace any longer remains. The ground at the site upon which the pyramid was to be constructed was marshy, and consequently a foundation of stupendous pillars was built for it. It was like an immense broad bridge. The pyramid was raised upon it. One could go around beneath it, as if into an immense temple formed of columns. It was divided off into innumerable rooms, dungeons, and spacious halls. The pyramid itself, up to the very summit, also contained numerous apartments, large and small, with openings like windows from which I saw cloths hanging and waving therein. All around the pyramid were baths and gardens. This building was the real center of Egyptian idolatry, astrology, witchcraft, and abominable impurity. Here children and the aged were offered in sacrifice. Astrologers and necromancers dwelt in the pyramid and there had their diabolical visions. From it they could look all around, both near and far.

Near the baths was immense machinery for purifying the muddy waters of the Nile. The baths witnessed the most infamous horrors of idol worship. I saw later on Egyptian women practicing the greatest abominations in them. I saw them employing all manner of methods to enhance their beauty (such as beauty was apparently conceived under these circumstances)—for example, to grow fat. After working up a sweat, female attendants would rub and massage them, opening their pores, after which they would bathe in chicken broth and all sorts of expensive spices, and then be rubbed with lard. These baths were in some way connected also with idolatrous debauchery.[1] This pyramid stood on the eastern bank of the Nile, not far from Memphis. It did not long exist, and was destroyed by someone, but I don't know who.[2]

I saw that the idols Osiris and Isis were no other than Joseph and Asenath, whose coming into Egypt the astrologers foresaw in their magical visions and confused dreaming. They consequently incorporated them into their religion. When they did come, they were honored and idolized as divinities. I saw that Asenath wept over such impiety and wrote against it. After Joseph and Asenath died, such idolization and dream experiences led to false images which, further misunderstood and twisted, were then written into their histories, all in so secret and intricate a way that no one knew any longer the when, where, or how of it all. The Egyptians thought they had lived just as they saw them portrayed in the stars, and since they had awaited their coming, they had venerated others who came earlier, whom they had mistaken for them (rather like the veneration of the false messiahs of the Jews).

---

[1] Elsewhere Anne Catherine says that Semiramis commissioned the construction of a peculiar pyramid in Egypt, and when it was completed, many baths were provided for the women, in connection with which child sacrifice and other atrocities were practiced—it all had to do with some sort of initiation.

[2] In related notes we read: "When Mary and Joseph fled to Egypt with Jesus I saw extraordinarily large buildings still around this city. Lower down than Memphis, not very far from the sea, lay the city of Saïs. I think it is still older than Memphis. Each of these four cities had its own king. Semiramis was very highly honored in Egypt, where, by her intrigues and diabolical arts, she greatly contributed to the spread of idolatry. I saw her in Memphis, where human sacrifices were common, plotting and practicing magic and astrology. I did not at this period see the bull Apis, but I saw idols with tails and a head like the sun. It was Semiramis who here planned the first pyramid; it was built on the eastern bank of the Nile, not far from Memphis. The whole nation had to assist at its construction. When it was completed I saw Semiramis again journeying thither with about two hundred followers. It was for the consecration of the building. Semiramis was honored almost as a divinity."

The nation was frightfully superstitious. The pagan priests were in darkness so great, and were so given to divination, that in Heliopolis even the dreams of the people were collected, recorded, and referred to the stars. According to their visions, idolatry was formulated, and even cycles of time computed, though, owing to the ignorance that had descended upon them, all manner of errors were introduced into these temporal reckonings. Their ambition in this was to take precedence over all other nations in point of time. With this end in view they drew up a number of complicated calendars and royal genealogical tables. By this, and frequent changes in their computations, order and true chronology were lost. Then, that this confusion might be firmly established, they perpetuated every error by inscriptions and the design of the great buildings they erected. For a long time they reckoned the ages of father and son, as if the date of the former's demise were that of the latter's birth. The kings, who waged constant war with the priests on the subject of chronology, inserted among their forefathers the names of persons that never existed. Thus the four kings of the same name who reigned simultaneously in Thebes, Hermopolis (its Egyptian name being Chmum), Memphis, and Saïs, were—in accordance with this ruse—reckoned one after the other.[1] I saw too that once they reckoned 970 days to a year, and then again sometimes years were computed as months. I cannot recall all the details. I saw a pagan priest, having taken some reckoning from the stars, drawing up a chronological table in which, for every five hundred years, eleven hundred were set down.

---

[1] On the subject of cities in ancient Egypt, Anne Catherine said: "The first was Thebes, then Chmum or Chemis [from Ham, or Chmuen]; another was Saïs; then Memphis as the most ancient—there being few other cities at the time of Semiramis than these four. In early days it was the practise of the priests of Chmum [said to be the same as is called by the Greeks Hermopolis] to go around in procession and write down each day all the dreams of the people, and in this connection also to look toward the alignment of the stars. Later arose much preoccupation with magnetism and devilish visions, both true and false; later still came a fascination with matters of all sorts pertaining to cycles of time, and the gods. At this time, these cities were not yet of the size they

I saw these false computations of the pagan priests at the same time that I beheld Jesus teaching on the sabbath at Aruma. Jesus, speaking before the Pharisees of the call of Abraham and his sojourn in Egypt, exposed the errors of the Egyptian calendar. He told them that the world had now existed 4028 years. When I heard Jesus say this, he was himself thirty-one years old.[1]

Scholars of the present day who write about Egypt are in gross error. They accept so many things concerning the Egyptians as history, science, and learning—which nevertheless have no other foundation than astrology and false visions—and in part subscribe to a similar bovine obtuseness in rejecting out of hand that such contorted inspirations and practices are possible. They esteem the Egyptians more ancient than they really are, because in those early times they appear to have possessed such knowledge of abstruse and hidden things.[2]

----

later attained, and the people did not live so close together in their settlements." On another occasion, regarding how Egypt was settled, Anne Catherine said (repeating some points already presented above): "This was achieved by many peoples, of which now one, now another, predominated. Those in the region of Thebes were quite distinctive, slender and light in color; those of Memphis and its surroundings short and stockier. The dark people with woolly hair were slaves already from the earliest times, and never rulers. It seems to me those who came early and built Thebes, crossed over from Africa. The others came over the Red Sea, entering Egypt as did the Israelites later. As for Chmum, it was later called Hermopolis [Magna], and lay well north of Thebes. At the time the Virgin Mary was in Egypt, I saw an extraordinarily large edifice there. Saïs lay further below Memphis [that is, to the north], not far from the sea, and it seemed to me it was a little older than the latter, which lay on the left bank of the Nile at a place where a great bridge spanned the river. On the right bank stood a castle in which lived the Pharaoh's daughter, who in one of the nearby watering-places discovered [the infant] Moses, who had been set adrift therein. It was on this side also that the pyramid of Semiramis had been built, which was later brought to ruin in a most unusual way, of which however I can recall no further details."

[1] When Anne Catherine said this, she added that Jesus was born in year 3997 of the world, and truly: 3997 + 31 = 4028.

[2] "I saw in those times, also, a people who honored Seth as a god. They made distant and perilous journeys into Arabia where they supposed his grave to be. It seems to me that the descendents of this people are still in existence,

Melchizedek was earlier among the folk whom the husband of Semiramis had pressed into slavery. He awoke some good people and to some extent set them apart, and comforted them. But then they were again enslaved.[1] Then I saw Melchizedek come as king of the morning star—that is, from the uttermost east—to the court of Semiramis in Babylon with a great retinue. Semiramis received him with great reverence but secretly dreaded him on account of his wisdom. She fancied he might perhaps woo her for his bride.

At this time it was not unusual for unknown sages or prophets from distant lands to appear, and when they did, they were much honored. In this way Melchizedek came to this region to visit several pious families among those peoples who had been captured, whom he then instructed and removed to other areas. Semiramis did not interfere, as she stood in fear of Melchizedek. These families did not grow into separate tribes but were settled in various places inhabited by more diminutive peoples, even quite wild ones, in order to support these latter, which through intermarriage would develop into a nobler race and thus come closer to a future salvation. Having established all these things, Melchizedek then departed.

But first Melchizedek spoke to Semiramis sternly, reproached her with her cruelty, and foretold to her the destruction of her pyramid at Memphis. Semiramis grew speechless from terror, and I saw the punishment that fell upon her. She became like a beast. She was for a long time penned up like a cow, and they cast to her in derision grass and straw in a manger; only one servant was faithful to her and furnished her with food. She was freed from the chastisement, but she carried on her disorders anew. She came at last to a frightful end, her intestines being torn from her body. She was aged one hundred and seventeen years.

---

and that the Turks suffer them to pass freely through their territory on their pilgrimages to that grave."

[1] Anne Catherine added that this tribe had occupied a region northeast of Babylon that lay beyond a great range of mountains and that this people is the same from whom later the great mage Zoroaster arose.

Semiramis reigned with indescribable grandeur and magnificence. She caused immense buildings to be erected by her slaves, whom she oppressed far more severely than did Pharaoh the children of Jacob in Egypt. The most horrible idolatry was practiced among the Babylonians. Human victims were buried up to the neck in the earth and thus offered in sacrifice. It is hardly credible to what a degree all kinds of luxury, magnificence, opulence, and the arts were carried. Semiramis also waged great wars; her armies were composed of countless warriors. But these wars were almost always against nations off toward the east. She went not much westward. The nations toward the north were dark and sinister-looking people.

ON Tuesday, May 1, AD 31, the disciples baptized while Jesus taught and healed the sick. He then began to teach the pagan philosophers about the nature of their cults and the arising of false gods. These philosophers had some intimation of the truth mixed up with faith in their own divinities, which they tried again to explain away by various interpretations. But all the personages and idols they wanted to explain had, in the course of time, become so mixed up and confused in their minds that even the cloud of Elijah and the Mother of God—of whom they knew nothing at all—had to be dragged by them into the general confusion. They called their goddess, Derketo, the queen of heaven. They spoke of her as of one that had brought to earth all that it had of wisdom and pleasure. They said that her followers having ceased to acknowledge her, she prophesied to them all that would befall them in the future; also that she would plunge into the sea and reappear as a fish to be with them forever. All this, they added, had actually come to pass. Her daughter, whom she had conceived in the sacred rites of paganism, was Semiramis,[1] the wise and powerful queen of Babylon. How wonderful!

While these men were thus speaking, I saw the whole history of

---

[1] As is depicted in the more detailed material presented above, Semiramis was the daughter of an unnamed daughter of Derketo, and thus Derketo's granddaughter.

these goddesses, as if they had really risen before me and were still alive. I felt impatient to disabuse the philosophers of their gross errors. They appeared to me so astonishingly silly in not seeing them themselves that I kept thinking: "Now, this is so distinct, so clear, that I will explain it all to them!" Then, again, I thought: "How dare you talk about such things! These learned men must know better than you!" and so I tormented myself during that conversation of several hours.

Melchizedek

WE have spoken of Melchizedek before and how I saw him as an angel and a type of Jesus, as a priest upon the earth, but also, inasmuch as the priesthood is in God, as an angel priest of the eternal hierarchy. I saw him preparing, founding, building up, and separating the human family, and acting toward them as a guide. Yes, I have often seen Melchizedek, but never as a human being. I have always seen him as a being of another nature, as an angel, as one sent by God.

I have never at any time seen any determinate dwelling place, any home, any family, any associates, connected with him. I never saw him eating, drinking, or sleeping; and never did the thought occur to me that he was a mortal. He was clothed as no priest at the time on the earth, but like the angels in the heavenly Jerusalem. His robes were such as Moses, upon the command of God, afterward ordained the priestly vestments should be. I have seen Melchizedek appearing here and there, interposing and legislating the affairs of nations; as, for instance, at the celebration of victories after war, at that time waged with such cruelty. Wherever he appeared, wherever he was, he exercised an irresistible influence by his mere presence. No one opposed him, and yet he never resorted to harsh measures; even the idolaters cheerfully accepted his decisions and acted upon his advice.

Melchizedek looked to me like a young man, perhaps twenty-four years of age. I have seen him active in many different times, but never did he seem any older. His appearance had not as much of the human to it as did that of Jesus. Never did I see him with his head covered. His hair was yellowish and full, flowing down behind his ears. Wherever he might be, he was as though the lord of that place. Often he was absent, and at such times it seemed to me he was in some other place than the earth, perhaps in paradise, or some other land of soul. Sometimes I beheld him traveling alone, at other times in the company of people and animals bearing some burden. Never did I see him accompanied by any like himself, whether a relation or a priest. When he labored and built in some spot, it seemed he was laying the foundation stone for a future grace, as though by his actions he was drawing attention to a particular location where something for the future was commencing. I had never thought upon such things, but am simply reporting what comes to me.

Melchizedek had no companion of his own nature; he was entirely alone. Sometimes he had two hired couriers. They were clothed in short white garments and they ran on before him to announce his coming. He dismissed them when their mission was over. All that he needed, he acquired without trouble. They from whom he received anything could always spare what they gave. They bestowed it upon him with joy. They regarded him with reverential fear, but esteemed themselves happy to be in his company. Although the wicked found fault with him, yet they humbled themselves in his presence. Melchizedek, that being of a higher order, was regarded by the great ones of the pagan world—those sensuous, godless men—in much the same light that an extraordinarily holy man would be looked upon at the present day if he suddenly appeared amongst us as a stranger doing good to all around.

Melchizedek and the Samanenses

THE *story of the deeds of Melchizedek at the time of Semiramis has already been told, up to the point where we now resume, learning of a people called by Anne Catherine the Samanenses whom Melchizedek led into Palestine, and what follows thereafter, regarding Abraham especially:*

For thirty years work on the tower of Babel had gone on. I saw one sent by God, Melchizedek, going around among the leaders and the masters of the building. He called upon them to account for their conduct and announced to them the chastisement of God, after which began the confusion. They formed parties, they laid claim to certain privileges. They struggled among themselves, they slew one another, they could no longer make themselves understood by one another, and so at last they separated and scattered over the whole earth. I saw Shem's race going farther southward where later on was Abraham's home. I saw one of Shem's race. He was a good man, but he did not follow his leader. On account of his wife, he preferred staying among the wicked ones of Babel. He became the leader of the Samanenses, a race that always held themselves aloof from others. Under the cruel Semiramis, Melchizedek transplanted them to Palestine.

Now, as time went on, there arose in the kingdom of Semiramis a numerous people of the Semitic race. After the building of the tower their ancestors had remained in Babylon. They lived as a little pastoral tribe under tents, raised cattle, and celebrated their religious ceremonies by night, either in an open tent or under the starry sky. Many blessings attended them, they were prosperous in all things, and their cattle were always remarkably fine. Semiramis, the diabolical woman, resolved to exterminate this tribe and she had already destroyed a great many belonging to it. She knew from the Blessing attending them that God had merciful designs over them; therefore would she, as an instrument of the devil, oppress them. When the distress of these people was at its height, Melchizedek appeared. He went to Semiramis, demanded permission for them to depart, and rebuked her for her cruelty. Semiramis yielded to his desires, and he led them in different bands toward Palestine. Melchizedek dwelt in a tent near Babylon, and here he broke that bread [see below] to the good people from which they received strength to depart. He pointed out to them, here and there in Canaan, places suitable for settlements, and they received from him land of various quality. He divided them off according to their purity in order than they should not mix with others. Their name sounded like Samanen, or Semanen. Melchizedek pointed out to some of them as suitable for a settlement the region that was afterward the site of the Dead Sea, but their city was destroyed with Sodom and Gomorrha.

Of the Samanenses whom Melchizedek settled in Palestine, I saw long before the coming of Abraham three men on the so-called bread mountain, in the neighborhood of Tabor. They lived in caves. They were of a browner complexion than Abraham and were clothed in skins. They bound a great leaf on their head to protect them from the sun. Their life, modeled on that of Enoch, was a holy one. Their religion was simple, though full of mysterious signification, and they had visions and revelations that they easily interpreted. Their religion taught that God would unite Himself with humankind, and for that union they must prepare in every possible way. They also offered sacrifice. A third part of their daily allowance they exposed to the sun, either to be consumed by it or perhaps for the benefit of other needy creatures. That the latter was the case, I also saw.

These people lived quite solitary, apart from the rest of the inhabitants of the country. The latter were not yet numerous and lived scattered here and there in abodes built in the style of fortified tent cities. I saw those three men going through the country digging wells, cutting down forests, and laying the foundations of subsequent cities. I saw them driving the evil spirits from the air around whole regions and banishing them to other places, to poor, swampy, foggy districts. I saw again that the wicked spirits prefer such wretched abodes. I often saw these men wrestling with them. At first I wondered how cities could arise where they laid stones which so soon became overgrown, and then I had another vision in which I was shown a number of places built on these sites, for instance: Saphat, Bethsaida, Nazareth (where those three men worked on the spot upon which afterward stood the house in which the angel delivered the message to Mary); Gath-Hepher, Sepphoris (in the region near Nazareth where Anne's house afterward stood); Megiddo, Nain, Ainon, and the caves of Bethlehem and Hebron. I also saw them founding Michmethath and many other places that I have now forgotten.

I saw them every month assembling on this mountain where Melchizedek broke a large four-cornered loaf (three feet square, perhaps, and tolerably thick) into numerous little pieces which he divided among them. The loaf was of a brownish color and had been baked in the ashes.

I saw that Melchizedek always went to them without a companion. Sometimes he bore the loaf quite lightly, as if it merely floated above his hand; and again, when he drew near to the mountain, I saw it as a weight upon his shoulders. I think he took this precaution on approaching them that they might look upon him as merely a man. Still, they met him with great reverence, prostrating before him. He taught them how to plant vines on Tabor. He also gave them all kinds of seeds, which they scattered in many parts of the country and which now grow wild there. I saw these people every day cutting a piece off the loaf with the brown spades they used at work. They also ate birds, which flew toward them in great numbers. They had festival days, and they were familiar with the stars. They celebrated the eighth day with prayer and sacrifice, also some days in the course of the year. I saw them also making numerous roads through the still wild country to the places where they had laid foundations, dug wells, and sowed seed. This they did, that the people coming after them might, by following these roads, make settlements near the wells and fertile places prepared for them. I saw these three men often surrounded while at work by crowds of evil spirits, whom they could see. I saw these spirits, by prayer and the word of command, banished to swampy wastes. They departed instantly, and the men went quietly on with their work, clearing and purifying. They made roads to Cana, Megiddo, and Nain, and in this way prepared the birthplace of most of the prophets. They laid the foundations of Abel-Mehola and Dothan, and dug out the beautiful baths at Bethulia. Melchizedek still scoured the country alone and as a stranger; no one knew where he lived.

The three Samanenses were old, but still very active. On the site of the Dead Sea and in Judea cities already existed. There were some also further north but none as yet in the central regions. The Samanenses dug their own graves and sometimes stretched themselves in them; one made his near Hebron, another on Tabor, and the third in the caves not far from Saphet. They were, in a certain sense, for Abraham what John was for Jesus. They purified the country, they prepared the land and the ways, they sowed good fruit, and they brought water for the leader of God's people. But John prepared the heart for penance and for a second birth in Jesus Christ. The Samanenses did for Israel what John did for the Church.

Melchizedek Marking Off the Land

I HAVE seen such men in other places also, where they had been introduced by Melchizedek. I often saw Melchizedek as he appeared in Palestine long before the time of Semiramis and Abraham, when the country was still a wilderness. He seemed to be laying it out, marking off and preparing certain districts. I saw him entirely alone, and I thought: "What is this man doing here so early? There is not a human being in this place!" I saw him near a mountain, boring a well—it was the source of the Jordan. He had a long fine instrument which, like a ray of light, pierced the mountainside. I saw him in the same way opening fountains in different parts of the earth. In those early times—that is, before the deluge—I never saw the rivers gushing forth and flowing as they do now, but I saw volumes of water pouring down from a high mountain in the east.[1]

Melchizedek took possession of many parts of Palestine by marking them off. He measured off the site for the pool of Bethesda, and long before Jerusalem existed he laid a stone where the Temple was to stand. I saw him planting in the bed of the Jordan the twelve precious stones upon which the priests stood with the Ark of the Covenant at the departure of the children of Israel. He planted them like seeds, and they increased in size. I always saw Melchizedek alone, save when he had to busy himself with the uniting, the separating, or the guiding of nations and families.

I saw that Melchizedek built a castle at Salem. But it was rather a tent with galleries and steps around it, like the castle of Mensor in Arabia. The foundation alone was solid, for it was of stone. I think the four corners where the principal posts stood were still to be seen even in John's time. It had only a very strong foundation of stone, which looked like a fortification overrun with verdure. John had there his little hut of rushes.

---

[1] See "Paradise" and "The Mountain of the Prophets."

That tent castle was a resort for strangers and travelers, a kind of safe and convenient inn near the pleasant waters. Perhaps Melchizedek, whom I have always seen as the guide and counselor of the still unsettled races and nations, kept this castle as a place in which to harbor and instruct them. But even at that time, it bore some reference to baptism.

This was Melchizedek's central point. From it he started on his journeys to lay out Jerusalem, to visit Abraham, and to go elsewhere. Here also he gathered together and distributed families and peoples, who settled in various places. All this took place previously to the offering of bread and wine which, I think, was made in a valley south of Jerusalem. Melchizedek built Salem before he built Jerusalem. Wherever he labored and constructed he seemed to be laying the foundation of a future grace, to be drawing attention to that particular place, to be beginning something that would be perfected in the future. Melchizedek belongs to the choir of angels that are set over countries and nations, that brought messages to Abraham and the other patriarchs. They stand opposite the Archangels Michael, Gabriel, and Raphael.

✝ ✝ ✝ ✝ ✝

ON the second day of the kings at the crib, lamps were already lighted when the kings took leave. They went out behind the hill toward the east to the field in which were their people and beasts. In it stood a high tree whose spreading boughs shaded a wide circumference. The tree was very old and had a legend of its own, for Abraham and Melchizedek had met under its branches. The shepherds and the people around regarded it as sacred. A spring gushed up before it, the waters of which the shepherds used at certain seasons on account of their healing qualities. There was near the tree a furnace that could be covered, and at both sides huts affording shelter at night. A hedge surrounded the whole tract. Thither went the kings and found all the followers still remaining to them gathered together. A light was suspended from the tree, and under it they prayed, and sang with indescribable sweetness.

At about the time John left the desert, the country around Salem and Ainon was as it were free, possessing a kind of privilege established by custom, by virtue of which the inhabitants dared not drive anyone from its borders. John had built his hut at Ainon on the old foundations of what was once a large building, but which had fallen to ruins and was now covered with moss and overgrown by weeds. Here and there arose a hut. These ruins were the foundations of the tent castle of Melchizedek. Of this place in particular I have had visions, all kinds of scenes belonging to early times, but I can now recall only this, that Abraham once had a vision here. He pulled two stones in position, one as an altar, and upon the other he knelt. I saw the vision that was shown to him—a City of God like the heavenly Jerusalem, and streams of water falling from the same. He was commanded to pray more for the coming of the City of God. The water streaming from the City spread around on all sides.

Abraham had this vision about five years before Melchizedek built his tent castle on the same spot. This castle was more properly a tent surrounded by galleries and flights of steps similar to Mensor's castle in Arabia. The foundation alone was solid; it was of stone. I think that even in John's time the four corners where the principal stakes once stood were still to be seen. On this foundation, which now looked like a mount overgrown with vegetation, John had built a little reed hut. The tent castle in Melchizedek's time was a public halting place for travelers, a kind of charming resting place by the pleasant waters. Jacob too had once lived at Ainon a long time with his herds. The cistern of the baptism pool was in existence at that early time, and I saw that Jacob repaired it. The ruins of Melchizedek's castle were near the water and the place of baptism; and I saw that in the early days of Christian Jerusalem a church stood on the spot were John had baptized. I saw this church still standing when Mary of Egypt passed that way when retiring into the desert.

With regard to the island upon which Jesus received baptism, which rose out of the Jordan, Anne Catherine reported that close to the edge of the well nearby was a three-cornered pyramidal stone resting on the sharp end. It was on this that Jesus was standing at his baptism when the Holy Spirit came upon him. On his right, and close to the edge of the well, arose the slender palm tree that he clasped during the baptism; on his left stood the Bap-

tist. This triangular stone upon which Christ Jesus stood was not
one of the twelve that surrounded the inside of the well. It seems
to me that they were precious stones that had been placed there
by Melchizedek before the waters of the Jordan had begun to
flow. But when he placed them there they were small. He had in
this way laid the foundations of many subsequent buildings.
These foundations had long lain concealed by mud and earth, but
when brought to light, they became holy places wherein something remarkable happened.

On Wednesday, October 12, AD 29, Jesus went to Succoth,
where he arrived toward evening. An innumerable multitude
gathered around him, among them many sick. He taught in the
synagogue and allowed Saturnin and four other disciples to
administer baptism. It took place at a spring in a rocky grotto fac-
ing westward toward the Jordan which, however, could not be
seen from it as a hill intervened. But the spring was fed from the
deep waters of the river. The light fell into the grotto from aper-
tures in the roof. In front of it was an extensive pleasure garden
beautifully laid out with small trees, aromatic shrubs, and well-
kept lawns. In it was an ancient memorial stone commemorative
of an apparition of Melchizedek to Abraham, who had once dwelt
at Succoth with his nurse Maraha, and had owned fields in three
different localities. Even here he had begun to share with Lot. It
was here that Melchizedek first appeared to Abraham in the same
way as did the angels. Melchizedek commanded him a threefold
sacrifice of doves, long-beaked birds, and other animals, promising to come again and offer bread and wine in sacrifice. He told
him what was going to happen to Sodom and to Lot, and pointed
out to him several graces for which he should pray. Melchizedek
at that time had no longer an earthly abode at Salem.

On Friday, October 21, AD 29, Jesus interpreted various passages from the scriptures to the friends gathered together and
thereafter consulted with them on the subject of his future
abode. He spoke of various places and of Melchizedek, whose
figurative priesthood was soon to be realized. Melchizedek had
laid out all the roads, founded all the places that in the designs of
God the Son of Man was afterward to travel over and evangelize.
Jesus concluded by telling them that he would be found mostly

around the Sea of Galilee. This conference was held in a retired apartment that opened upon a garden attached to the baths.

On Tuesday, January 17, AD 30, Jesus went with several of his disciples southward from the place of baptism and toward the west of the Dead Sea. He had entered the region in which Melchizedek sojourned when he measured off the Jordan and the mountains. Long before Abraham, he had conducted the patriarch's forefathers thither. But the city that they built had been destroyed with Sodom and Gomorrha. Where now appears the Dead Sea was before the submersion of those godless cities only the river Jordan. The remote ancestors of Abraham, who had been settled in Hazezon by Melchizedek, had become very degenerate, and Abraham was, by a second exercise of God's mercy, led to the promised land. Melchizedek had been in these parts long before the Jordan existed. He had measured off and determined everything. He often came and went, and sometimes he was accompanied by a couple of men, who appeared to be slaves.

On Wednesday, October 11, AD 30, Jesus and the disciples arrived at the town of Salem early in the afternoon. The Salemites took Jesus to their beautiful fountain and tendered to him the customary refreshments. There were gathered around the fountain numbers of sick of all kinds, so numerous that even the streets were lined with them. Jesus at once began to cure, passing quietly from one to another until nearly four o'clock, when he assisted at a dinner given at an inn, and thence proceeded to the synagogue to preach. During the discourse he spoke of Melchizedek, also of Malachi who had once sojourned here and who had prophesied the sacrifice according to the Order of Melchizedek. Jesus told them that the time for that sacrifice was drawing near, and that those ancient prophets would have been happy to have seen and heard what they now saw and heard.

Throughout the sabbath on Saturday, September 6, AD 32, Jesus taught concerning the vine, the grain, bread, and wine. He spoke of Melchizedek as a forerunner, whose sacrifice was bread and wine; in himself, however, the sacrifice had become flesh and blood. Jesus indicated clearly that he was the messiah, and said that they should follow him.

From Monday, September 22, to Wednesday, September 24,

AD 32, during Jesus's extended visit to the two of the three kings [Mensor and Theokeno] still living at that time, Mensor went with Jesus to Theokeno, who on account of weakness and old age was no longer able to walk. Mensor and Theokeno related how they had seen the star that led them to the newborn child in Bethlehem. They asked Jesus why they had lost sight of the star as they had approached Jerusalem. Jesus replied: "To test your faith, and because it should not come across Jerusalem." With this, Jesus said that he was not the envoy of the king of the Jews but was himself that king. He added that he had come for Gentiles as well as for Jews, for all who believed in him.

Now, the kings had some knowledge of Abraham and David; and when Jesus spoke of his ancestors, they produced some old books and searched in them to see whether they too could not claim descent from the same race. The books were in the form of tablets opening out in a zigzag form, like sample patterns. Then they told him that they knew something of Melchizedek and his sacrifice of bread and wine, and said that they too had a sacrifice of the same kind, namely, a sacrifice of little leaves and some kind of a green liquor. When they offered it they spoke some words like these: "Whoever eats me and is devout shall have all kinds of felicity." Jesus told them that Melchizedek's sacrifice was a type of the most holy sacrifice, and that he himself was the victim. Thus, though plunged in darkness, these pagans had preserved many forms of truth. On another occasion, as the kings, as was said, had some knowledge of Melchizedek, they again questioned Jesus concerning his sacrifice. And when he blessed the bread for them, he gave them some idea of his passion and of the Last Supper.

The large chalice used at the Last Supper once belonged to Abraham. Melchizedek brought it from the land of Semiramis, where it was lying neglected, to the land of Canaan, when he began to mark off settlements on the site afterward occupied by Jerusalem. He had used it at the sacrifice of bread and wine offered in Abraham's presence, and he afterward gave it to him. This same chalice was even in Noah's possession. It stood in the upper part of the ark. Moses also had it in his keeping. The Cup was massive like a bell. It looked as if it had been shaped by nature, not formed by art. I have seen clear through it. Jesus alone knew of what it was made.

I do not remember having seen the Master himself receive the sacred species. I must have let that pass unnoticed. When he administered his body and blood to the apostles, it appeared to me as if he emptied himself, as if he poured himself out in tender love. It is inexpressible. Neither did I see Melchizedek, when sacrificing bread and wine, receive it himself. It was given me to know why priests partake of the sacrifice, although Jesus did not.

After the following excursus on Job, in the subsequent section on Abraham, we shall return to Melchizedek as he offers the sacrifice of bread and wine, at which time Abraham receives the sacrament of the Old Covenant.

Job

JOB was the youngest of thirteen brothers. His father was a great chieftain at the time of the building of the tower of Babel. His father had one brother, who was Abraham's ancestor. The tribes of these two brothers generally intermarried. Job's first wife was of the tribe of Peleg.[1] She was at first a good wife to him, but thereafter took a turn for the worse. After many adventures, when he was living in his third home, Job married three more wives of the same tribe. One of them bore him a son whose daughter married into the tribe of Peleg and gave birth to Abraham's mother. Job was thus the great-grandfather of Abraham's mother. Job may have still been alive at the time of Abraham's birth.[2] Job's father was called Joktan, a son of Heber. He lived to the north of the Cas-

---

[1] Peleg (Phaleg, Phalek), according to the Hebrew bible, was one of the two sons of Eber (Heber), an ancestor of the Israelites. The other son was Joktan.

[2] The book of Job gives no clue to the ancestry, offspring, or homeland of Job, and (as Anne Catherine remarks elsewhere) it is difficult to recognize the true history of Job from it. Job is only mentioned elsewhere in the Old Testament as a just man, together with Noah and Daniel (Ezekiel 14:14, 16, 20). Rabbinic lore has, however, many accounts of the circumstances of Job's family; some texts place Job as a contemporary of Abraham, while others place him earlier or later. There are several accounts of his visit to Egypt.

113

pian Sea, near a mountain range one side of which is quite warm, while the other is cold and ice-covered. There were elephants in that country. I do not think elephants could have gone to the place where Job first went to set up his own tribe, for it was very swampy there [see below]. Job could not remain in his parents' house. His ideas and inclinations did not accord with theirs. Job adored in nature the One Only God, especially in the stars and in the change from day to night. He spoke frequently of God's wonderful works, and offered to Him a worship purer than that of those around him.

Job moved with his followers to a place north of a mountain range [the Caucasus] lying between two seas, the westernmost of which was before the deluge a high mountain inhabited by evil angels by whom men were possessed.[1] The country there was poor and marshy, so much so that travel there was difficult.[2] I think it is now inhabited by a nation distinguished by their flat noses, high cheekbones, and small eyes. Here Job first settled, and things went well with him. He gathered around him all kinds of poor, abandoned creatures who dwelt in caves and bushes, and who lived exclusively upon the raw flesh of birds and animals taken in hunting. Job was the first who taught them how to cook their food. With their help he dug up and cultivated the land. He and his people wore at that time but little clothing and dwelt in tents.

Job soon found himself the owner of immense herds in this place, among them numerous striped asses and spotted animals. Once three sons were born to him at one birth, and three daughters at another. He had as yet no city here, but went around among his fields, which extended to a distance of seven leagues. No grain was cultivated in those marshy districts; but they raised a large sedge, which grows also in water, and whose pith was

---

[1] It is remarkable that Anne Catherine said on another occasion that the Caspian Sea had been before the deluge a high mountain on which evil angels held sway. This seems to show that the mountain range behind which Job's first dwelling-place was situated must have been the Caucasus. CB

[2] It was here that Job's first misfortune befell him, and he then moved southward to the Caucasus and began his life anew.

eaten either boiled or roasted. They dried their meat in holes dug in the earth, and exposed to the sun, until Job taught them how to cook it. They planted many species of gourds for food.

Job was, to be sure, a pagan, be he was unspeakably gentle, affable, just, and benevolent. He assisted all in need. He was, too, exceedingly pure and very familiar with God, who communicated with him through an angel, or "a white man," as the people of that period expressed it. These angelic apparitions were like radiant, but beardless, youths (in appearance perhaps twenty years of age) in long white garments that fell in heavy folds or strips around them, I could not distinguish which.[1] They were girded, and they took food and drink.

God consoled Job during his sufferings by means of these apparitions, and they passed sentence on his friends, his nephews, and his other relatives. He did not, like the nations around him, worship idols. They made for themselves images of all kinds of animals and adored them. But Job fabricated for himself a representation of the almighty God, the figure of a child crowned with rays, and I think it had wings. The hands were held one above the other, and in one was a globe upon which was depicted a little vessel riding on the waves. I think it was to represent the deluge, of which—as well as of the wisdom and mercy of God—Job often spoke to his two confidential servants. The figure was portable and shone like metal. Job prayed before it and burned grain before it as a sacrifice. The smoke arose from the top of it as through a funnel. Figures of this kind were afterwards introduced into Egypt, sitting in a kind of pulpit with a canopy above.

It was in this place that Job's first affliction befell him. The time that intervened between the different misfortunes recorded of him was not for him a time of peace. He always had to combat and struggle against the wicked races by whom he was surrounded. After his first affliction he removed further up the mountain range, the Caucasus, where he again began anew and where prosperity again followed him. He and his followers now

---

[1] In this respect they were similar to Melchizedek, but that they were without beard.

began to clothe themselves less scantily, and their mode of life exhibited more refinement.

From this, his second dwelling place, Job made a great expedition to Egypt, a land which at that time was ruled by foreign kings belonging to a shepherd people from Job's fatherland. One of these came from Job's own country, another came from the farthest country of the three holy kings. They ruled over only a part of Egypt and were later driven out by an Egyptian king.[1] At one time there was a great number of these shepherd people all collected together in one city; they had migrated to Egypt from their own country. The king of these shepherds from Job's country desired a wife for his son from his family's tribe in the Caucasus, and Job brought this royal bride (who was related to him) to Egypt with a great following. He had thirty camels with him, and many menservants and rich presents.

When I saw him in Egypt, Job was a large, powerful man of agreeable appearance; he had a yellowish-brown complexion and reddish hair. Abraham was fairer. The Egyptians were of an earthy brown. At that time Egypt was not thickly populated; only here and there were large masses of people. There were no great buildings either; these did not appear until the time of the children of Israel.

Job found a terrible form of idolatry here in this city, descending from the pagan magical rites practiced at the building of the tower of Babel. They had an idol with a broad ox's head rising to a point at the top. Its mouth was open, and behind its head were twisted horns. Its body was hollow, fire was made in it, and live children were thrust into its glowing arms. I saw something being taken out of holes in its body. The people here were horrible, and the land full of dreadful beasts. Great black creatures with fiery manes flew about in swarms, scattering what seemed like fire as they flew. They poisoned everything in their path and the trees withered away under them. I saw other animals with long hind-legs and short fore-legs, like moles; they could leap from roof to

---

[1] The Hyksos or "shepherd kings" were foreign rulers in Egypt, c. 1730–1580 BC, who were finally driven out by a native dynasty.

roof. Then there were frightful creatures lurking in hollows and between stones, which wound themselves around men and strangled them. In the Nile I saw a heavy, awkward beast with hideous teeth and thick black feet. It was the size of a horse and had something pig-like about it. Besides these I saw many other ugly creatures, but the people here were much more horrible than any of them. Job, whom I saw clearing the evil beasts from around his dwelling by his prayers, had such a horror of these godless folk that he often broke out in loud reproaches of them, saying he would rather live with all these dreadful beasts than with the infamous inhabitants of this land.

I often saw Job at sunrise gazing longingly toward his own country, which lay a little to the south of the farthest country of the three holy kings. Job saw prophetic pictures foreshadowing the arrival in Egypt of the children of Israel; he also had visions of the salvation of humankind and of the trials that awaited himself. He would not be persuaded to stay in Egypt, and at the end of five years he and his companions left the country.

As was said, there were intervals of calm between the great misfortunes that befell Job: the first interval lasted nine years, the second seven, and the third twelve. The words in the book of Job (1:16–18): "And while he (the messenger of evil) was yet speaking" mean "This misfortune of his was still the talk of the people when the following befell him." His misfortunes came upon him in three different places. The last calamity—and also the restoration of all his prosperity—happened when he was living in a flat country directly to the east of Jericho. Water was scarce, but incense and myrrh were found here, and there was also a gold mine dug into the red earth, with smithies. But he never was so absolutely ruined as to have nothing left; he merely became quite poor as compared with his former circumstances. He always had enough left to pay his debts.

The shepherd king for whose son Job conducted the bride into Egypt would fain have kept him there, and he assigned to him Matarea as a dwelling place. The region was at that time very different from what it was at a later period when the holy family sojourned there. Still, I saw that Job dwelt on the spot afterward occupied by them, and that the spring of Mary was already shown him by God.[1] When Mary discovered this spring it was already lined with stone, though still covered over. Job used the great stone by the well for religious worship. By prayer he freed the country around his dwelling place from wild and venomous animals. Further visions referring to humankind's salvation were vouchsafed him here, and he saw too, as before, the trials in store for him. With burning zeal he exclaimed against the infamous practices of the Egyptians and their human sacrifices. I think these latter were in consequence abolished.

It was when Job had returned to his native country that his second misfortune overtook him; and when, after twelve years of peace, the third came upon him, he was living more toward the south and directly eastward from Jericho. I think this country had been given him after his second calamity, because he was everywhere greatly revered and loved for his admirable justice, his knowledge, and his fear of God. This country was a level plain, and here Job began afresh. On a height, which was very fertile, noble animals of various kinds were running around, also wild camels. They caught them in the same way as we do the wild horses on the heath.

Job settled on this height. Here he prospered, became very rich, and built a city. The foundations were of stone; the dwellings were tents. It was during this period of great prosperity that his third calamity, his grievous distemper, overtook him. After enduring this affliction with great wisdom and patience he entirely recovered, and again became the father of many sons and daughters. I think Job did not die till long after, when another nation intruded itself into the country.

Although in the book of Job this narrative is given very differently, yet many of Job's own words are therein recorded. I think I

---

[1] On another occasion, tracing the history of the spring in question, Anne Catherine said: "The spring that appeared at Matarea in answer to the Blessed Virgin's prayers was not a new one, but an old one, which gushed forth afresh. It had been choked, but was still lined with masonry. I saw that Job had been in Egypt long before Abraham and had dwelt on this spot also (as did Abraham later). It was he who found the spring and he made sacrifices on the great stone lying here." See "The Spring at Matarea" in *Inner Life and Worlds of Soul & Spirit* and "Mary Discovers a Spring Near Their House" in *The Life of the Virgin Mary.*

could distinguish them all. Where the story says that the servants came quickly one after another to Job with news of his losses, it must be remarked that the words "And as he still spoke of it" signify "And while the last calamity was not yet effaced from the mind of men," etc.

That satan appeared before God with the sons of God, and brought an action against Job is told in this way only for the sake of brevity. There was at that time much communication between the evil spirits and idolaters to whom they appeared in angelic form. In this way satan incited his wicked neighbors against Job, and they calumniated him. They said that he did not serve God properly, that he had a superfluity of possessions, and that it was very easy for him to be good. Then God resolved to show that afflictions are often only trials, etc.

The friends who spoke around Job symbolized the reflections of his kinsmen upon his fate. But Job longingly awaited the Savior, and he was one of the ancestors of the race of David. He was to Abraham, through the mother of the latter (who was one of his descendants), what the ancestors of Anne were to Mary.

The history of Job, together with his dialogues with God, was circumstantially written down by two of his most trusty servants, who seemed to be his stewards.[1] They wrote upon bark, and from Job's own dictation. These two servants were named, respectively, Hay and Uis (or Ois). These narratives were held very sacred by Job's descendants. They passed from generation to generation down to Abraham. In the school of Rebecca, the Canaanites were instructed in them on account of the lessons of submission under trials from God that they inculcated.

Through Jacob and Joseph they descended to the children of Israel in Egypt. Moses collected and arranged them differently for the use of the Israelites during their servitude in Egypt and their painful wanderings in the wilderness; for they contained many details that might not have been understood and that would have been of no service in his time. But Solomon again entirely remodeled them, omitting many things and inserting others of his own.

---

[1] In 1835 the writer heard that the founder of the Armenian race was so named. CB

And so this once authentic history became a sacred book made up of the wisdom of Job, Moses, and Solomon. One can now only with difficulty trace the particular history of Job, for the names of cities and nations were assimilated to those of the land of Canaan, on which account Job came to be regarded as an Edomite.

Other References to Job

I HEARD that the three kings traced their genealogy back to Job, who had dwelt on the Caucasus and had jurisdiction over other districts far and wide. Long before Balaam, and before Abraham's sojourn in Egypt, they had the prophecy of the star and the hope of its fulfillment. The leaders of a race from the land of Job had—upon an expedition to Egypt, in the region of Heliopolis—received from an angel the revelation that from a Virgin the Savior would be born whom their descendants would honor. They were also instructed to go no farther, but to return to their homes and watch the stars.

The children of that time were sometimes placed in shallow water, remaining there for some time while covered with an awning. In this state those around them beheld all manner of things from which Job was able to prophesy regarding their destiny. Job also searched for the marks of his children, and from certain birthmarks gained foreknowledge of their destiny—as did also later patriarchs. For example, Jacob bore such a birthmark, from which his mother understood to give him precedence over [his brother] Esau. The children of kings and prophets often bore such birthmarks also—for instance David, Saul, etc.—on account of which they were recognized and chosen.

I saw Job in Arabia dressed in a broad cloak, sitting upon an enormous heap of straw. His friends were at some distance, and roundabout were huts set beneath trees. These friends were placed upon his lap naked as children, as though being adopted [by him].

ON Tuesday, August 29, AD 30, Jesus and his disciples visited a school for orphans in Abel-Mehola, where he told the children the story of Job as it actually took place.[1] At the moment of Jesus's entrance into this school the boys were making some calculation connected with Job. As they could not readily do it, Jesus explained it and wrote it down for them in letters. He also explained to them something relating to measure, two hours of distance or time, I do not now know which. He explained much of the book of Job. Some of the rabbis at this period attacked the truth of the history therein contained, since the Edomites, to which race Herod belonged, bantered and ridiculed the Jews for accepting as true the history of a man of the land of Edom, although in that land no such man was ever known to exist. They looked upon the whole story as a mere fable, gotten up to encourage the Israelites under their afflictions in the desert.

But Jesus related Job's history to the boys as if it had really happened. He did so in the manner of a prophet and catechist, as if he saw all passing before him, as if it were his own history, as if he heard and saw everything connected with it, or as if Job himself had told it to him. His hearers knew not what to think. Who was this man that now addressed them? Was he one of Job's contemporaries? Or was he an angel of God? Or was he God himself? But the boys did not wonder long about it, for they soon felt that Jesus was a prophet, and they associated him with Melchizedek, of whom they had heard and of whose origin man knows not.

---

[1] Anne Catherine says elsewhere that Job was Abraham's great-great-great-grandfather.

Job Hears Bad Tidings

The Patriarchs
and Their Families

Abraham
(Sarah, Hagar, Isaac, Ishmael)

ABRAHAM and his forefathers belonged to a very peculiar type of a mighty race. They led a pastoral life. They were not really natives of Ur, in Chaldea, but had removed there. They exercised special authority and jurisdiction. Here and there they took possession of certain regions where good pasturage was found. They marked off the boundaries, erected an altar of stones, and the land thus enclosed became their property.

Something happened to Abraham in his early childhood similar to that which occurred to the child Moses, by which his nurse saved his life. It had been prophesied to the ruler of the country that a wonderful child would be born whose birth would be very fatal to his interests. The ruler took measures accordingly, on which account Abraham's mother concealed herself before his birth in the same cave in which Seth had been hidden by Eve. There Abraham was born, and there secretly reared by his nurse Maraha. She passed for a poor slave who worked in the wilderness. Her hut was near this cave, which was named after her the milk cave. She was, after her death and in accordance with her own request, buried there by Abraham.

Abraham was a remarkably large child. When, on account of his unusual size, he was of an age to pass for a child born before the prophecy alluded to, his parents took him home. But his precocious wisdom exposed him to danger, so the nurse fled with him, and again concealed him a long time in the same cave. Many children of his age were massacred at that time. Abraham tenderly loved Maraha, his nurse. In after years, in all his wanderings he took her with him on a camel. She also dwelt with him at

Succoth. She died at the age of one hundred years. Abraham hewed out a tomb for her in the white stone which, like a hill, enclosed the cave in which he was born. The cave became a place of devotion, especially for mothers. Throughout the whole of this history, we discover a mysterious prefiguring of the early persecutions which Mary with the child Jesus had to endure. It was, too, in this same cave that they hid from Herod's soldiers when they sought the child.

The father of Abraham received great graces from heaven, and understood many mysteries. His people were nomads, and possessed the gift of discovering gold in the earth, and he fabricated out of it little idols similar to those that Rachel purloined from Laban. Ur is a place in the north of Chaldea. I perceived in many parts of this region, on mountains and plains, white flames arising, as if the ground were on fire. I know not whether this fire was spontaneous or kindled by man.

Abraham was a great astronomer. He understood the properties of things, and the influence of the stars upon birth. He saw all kinds of things in the stars, but he turned all to God. He followed God in all things and served him alone. He imparted his knowledge to others in Chaldea, but he traced all back to God.

I saw that in a vision he received from God the order to depart from his own country. God showed him another land, and Abraham next morning, without asking any questions, led forth all his people and departed. I afterward saw him pitching his tent in a region of Palestine that seemed to me to lie around the place where Nazareth subsequently stood. Abraham himself erected here an oblong altar of stone with a tent over it.

Once when kneeling before the altar, a light descended from heaven upon him. An angel, a messenger from God, appeared, said something to him, and presented to him a shining, transparent gift. The angel spoke with Abraham, and the latter received the mysterious Blessing, the Holy Thing from heaven; he opened his garment and laid it upon his breast. I was told that this was the sacrament of the Old Testament. Abraham, as yet, knew not what it contained. It was hidden from him, as from us is concealed the substance of the most holy sacrament. But it was given to him as a Sacred Thing, as a pledge of the promised posterity. The angel was exactly of the same kind as the one that announced to the Blessed Virgin the conception of the messiah. He was also as gentle and tranquil as Gabriel in the execution of his commission, not so hasty and rapid as I see other angels under similar circumstances. I think Abraham always carried the mysterious Gift about with him. The angel spoke to him of Melchizedek, who was to celebrate before him the sacrifice which, after the coming of the messiah, would be accomplished, and which should be continued forever. Abraham then took from a casket five large bones which he laid upon the altar in the form of a cross. A light burned before it, and he offered sacrifice. The fire burned like a star, the center white and the rays red.

In the intervals between the visions of the three days during which I saw what was happening on that wide pasture land [along the route taken by the three kings], I was shown much about the places in which Abraham lived, but have forgotten most of it. Once, in the distance, I saw the mountain on which Abraham was preparing to sacrifice Isaac. Another time I was shown very clearly Hagar and Ishmael in the desert, although this happened a long way from here. I cannot remember in what connection this was.

When Abraham was in Egypt, for a time he had his tents beside the spring of Matarea,[1] and I saw him teaching the people here.[2] He lived in the country several years with Sarah and a number of his sons and daughters whose mothers had remained behind in Chaldea. His brother Lot was also here with his family, but I do not remember what place of residence was assigned to him.[3] He went thither in obedience to a command from God; firstly because of a famine in the land of Canaan, and secondly to fetch a family treasure that had found its way to Egypt through a niece of Sarah's mother. This niece was of the race of the shep-

---

[1] See page 118, note 1.

[2] Flavius Josephus (lib. I, *Antiquitat. Jud.*, c. 8) and others state that Abraham instructed the Egyptians in arithmetic and astrology. CB

[3] Abraham in Egypt: Gen. 12:13. That Lot was with him is shown by 13:1. That Abraham taught the Egyptians is an old Jewish tradition, preserved in Josephus, *Ant.*, I, viii, 2; and there are many Rabbinic stories about his sojourn in Egypt, especially in the Midrash (e.g., *Genesis Rabba,* XLI and XLIV).

herd-people [the Hyksos] belonging to Job's tribe who had been rulers of part of Egypt. She had gone there to be serving maid to the reigning family and had then married an Egyptian. She was also the foundress of a tribe, but I have forgotten its name. Hagar, the mother of Ishmael, was a descendant of hers and was thus of Sarah's family.[1] The woman had carried off this family treasure just as Rachel had carried off Laban's household gods, and had sold it in Egypt for a great sum. In this way it had come into the possession of the king and the priests. Abraham's first dwelling-place was high up, and the lands of the three kings were below and around it.

I will here describe the picture of Ishmael and Hagar.[2] At the side of Abraham's mountain, more towards the lower part of the valley, I saw Hagar and her son wandering about in the bushes; she seemed quite beside herself. The boy was only a few years old and was wearing a long dress. His mother was wrapped in a long cloak that covered her head; under it she wore a short dress, the upper part of which was tight round her body; and her arms, too, were tightly wrapped round. She laid the child under a tree on a hill, and made signs on his forehead, on the middle of his right

---

[1] Anne Catherine says elsewhere of Hagar: "Hagar was a descendent of the maid from Sarah's kin who had sold the genealogical table in Egypt, and had married an Egyptian. With the words 'I want to build myself [to have a child] out of her' Sarah [when she was barren] expressed that she considered Hagar a vessel of her tribe when she took her to Abraham. She felt herself as a female blossom united with all the other female blossoms of her kin, and imagined to impregnate herself in Hagar. At that time everything felt like one tree, as if the blossom was from the same trunk. To Sarah, that is, Hagar was a vessel, or flower, of her tribe, and she hoped for a fruit of her tribe from her."

On one occasion Anne Catherine had a vision of Hagar as a presentiment of the cross in the Old Testament, as follows: "I had a very distinct vision of Hagar after she was cast out. I understood that as she laid her son Ishmael under the tree she made a sign, a letter, upon his forehead, at the midpoint of his upper arms, both right and left, and upon his chest, after which she raised her eyes on high as she turned around. I saw the letters thus traced upon Ishmael grow bright, and then a spring of water gush forth. I had the sense that all this pointed to the cross."

[2] Hagar and Ishmael: Gen. 21:14–21.

upper arm, on his breast, and on his left upper arm. When she went away I did not see the mark on his forehead, but the other marks, which had been made on his clothing, remained visible as if drawn in red-brown color. These marks were in the form of a cross, but not an ordinary one. They were like a Maltese cross, only the points of the four triangles were arranged in the shape of a cross around a ring. In the four triangles she wrote signs or letters, like hooks, whose significance I could not clearly retain in my mind; I saw her also write two or three letters in the ring, in the middle. She drew this very rapidly with some red color that she seemed to have in her hand (or perhaps it was blood). As she did this she kept her thumb and forefinger pressed together.

Thereupon she turned round, gazed up to heaven, and did not look around again at her son. She went about a gun shot's distance away and sat down under a tree. She heard a voice from heaven, rose up, and went farther away. Again she heard a voice, and saw a spring of water under the leaves. She filled her leather water-bottle at the spring, and going back to her son gave him to drink and led him to the spring, where she put another garment over the one she had marked with crosses.

That is what I remember of this vision. I think I saw Hagar in the desert twice before, once before the birth of her son, and the second time with the young Ishmael as now.

This treasure[1] was a genealogy of the children of Noah (especially of the children of Shem) down to Abraham's time. It looked

like a scales hanging on several chains from inside a lid. This lid was made to shut down onto a sort of box that enclosed the chains in it. The chains were made of triangular pieces of gold linked together; the names of each generation were engraved on these pieces, which were thick yellow coins, while the links connecting them were pale like silver and thin. Some of the gold pieces had a number of others hanging from them. The whole

---

[1] Mentioned just above in connection with a niece of Sarah's mother, of whom Hagar was a descendent.

treasure was bright and shining. I heard, but have forgotten, what was its value in shekels. The Egyptian priests had made endless calculations in connection with this genealogy, but never arrived at the right conclusion.

Before Abraham came into their country, the Egyptians must have known—from their astrologers and from the prophecies of their sorceresses—that he and his wife came from the noblest of races and that he was to be the father of a chosen people. They were always searching in their prophetic books for noble races, and tried to intermarry with them. This gave satan the opportunity of attempting to debase the pure races by leading the Egyptians astray into immorality and deeds of violence.

Abraham, fearing that he might be murdered by the Egyptians because of the beauty of Sarah, his wife, had given out that she was his sister. This was not a lie, since she was his stepsister, the daughter of his father Terah by another wife [see Gen. 20:12]. The Pharaoh caused Sarah to be brought into his palace and wished to take her to wife. Abraham and Sarah were then in great distress and besought God for help. Thereafter, whenever Pharaoh approached Sarah with impure intentions, he would fall sick, or faint, and all his wives and most of the women in the city fell ill. Pharaoh, in alarm, caused inquiry to be made, and when he heard that Sarah was Abraham's wife, he gave her back to him, begging him to leave Egypt as soon as possible. It was clear, he said, that Abraham and his wife were under the protection of the gods.

The Egyptians were a strange people. On the one hand they were extremely arrogant and considered themselves to be the greatest and wisest among the nations. On the other hand they were excessively cowardly and servile, and gave way when they were faced by a power they feared was greater than theirs. This was because they were not sure of all their knowledge, most of which came to them in dark, ambiguous sooth-sayings, which easily produced conflicts and contradictions. Since they were very credulous of wonders, any such contradiction at once caused them great alarm.

And so, when Abraham had come to Pharaoh in great humility, calling him a father of peoples in famine, he called forth immediately the Pharaoh's goodwill. It was then that his wife Sarah had been brought to Pharaoh. But as has been said, Pharaoh fell ill at the time, and all his wives, indeed most all of the women in the city, were in their time of bleeding. And so Pharaoh courteously returned to Abraham his wife, expressing his wish that they return whence they had come, the sooner the better. It was then that Abraham responded that he could not leave without the treasure, the genealogical table—relating to him then the whole story of why he had come. Pharaoh called then his priests together and gladly gave to Abraham what he had come for, asking only that they be allowed to make a copy, to which Abraham agreed.

When Pharaoh was visited by heavy afflictions he consulted with his idolatrous priests, and granted to Abraham all he demanded. Upon Abraham's return to Palestine I saw Lot by him in a tent. Abraham was pointing all around with his hand. In his bearing there was something of the deportment of the three kings. He wore a long white, woolen garment with sleeves; a plaited white girdle with tassels; and a sort of cowl hanging down the back. On his head was a small cap and upon his breast a shield in the shape of a heart made of metal or precious stones. His beard was long.

I have no words to say how kind and generous Abraham was. If he had anything that pleased another, especially if it were cattle, he offered it to him at once, for he was a declared enemy to envy and covetousness. Lot's clothing was almost like that of Abraham, but he was not so tall, nor so noble-looking. He was indeed good, but at the same time a little covetous. I often saw the servants of the two disputing, and I saw Lot separating from Abraham. But as he went, I saw him enveloped in fog. Over Abraham I saw light. I saw him take down his tents and wander about. He built an altar of field stones and raised a tent over it. The people of that time were skillful in building out of rough stones, and the master with the servant put his hand to the work.

The altar just mentioned was in the region of Hebron, the subsequent dwelling place of Zechariah, the father of the Baptist. The region to which Lot removed was very good, as was all this part of the country toward the Jordan. I saw the cities around Lot's dwelling place plundered, and Lot himself with all his goods and chattels carried off. I saw a fugitive bear the news to Abraham, who immediately invoked the aid of heaven. Then, gathering his servants together, he surprised the enemy and freed his brother. The latter thanked him gratefully and was full of regret for having separated from him.

The enemy and the warriors in general, especially the giants, were not clothed like Abraham's followers. Their garments were narrower and shorter; their dress was in many pieces, covered with buttons, stars, and ornaments of other kinds. The giants were extraordinarily large people. They brutally and insolently carried off all they could lay their hands upon, but they were often obliged to yield their booty to others who plundered them in turn.

Melchizedek's Sacrifice of Bread and Wine

I OFTEN saw Melchizedek with Abraham. He appeared to him in the same way as did the angels at different times. Once he commanded of him a triple sacrifice of doves and other birds, and he prophesied concerning Sodom and Lot. He told him that he would come to him again to sacrifice bread and wine, and indicated to him, also, for what he should pray to God. Abraham was full of reverence before Melchizedek, and he eagerly awaited the promised sacrifice. As a preparation for it he built a very beautiful altar and surrounded it with an arbor. When about to come for the sacrifice of bread and wine, Melchizedek sent messengers to command Abraham to make his coming known and to announce him as the king of Salem. Abraham went out to meet him. He knelt before him and received his Blessing.[1] Melchizedek's sacrifice took place in a valley lying to the south of the fruited valley of vineyards running up to Gaza.

Melchizedek came from the region where Jerusalem afterward stood. He had with him a very nimble animal of a gray color. It had a short, broad neck and it was laden on both sides. On one

---

[1] See pages 124–25 for a fuller account of the transfer of the mysterious Blessing from the messenger of God to Abraham.

was a vessel of wine, flat on the side that lay against the beast; on the other was a box containing rows of flat, oval loaves, likewise the chalice that I afterward saw used at the Last Supper for the institution of the blessed sacrament. It had cups in the shape of little barrels. These vessels were of neither gold nor silver, but transparent as of brownish precious stones. They did not appear to me to have been fabricated by human art; rather, they looked as if they had grown.

The impression made by Melchizedek was similar to that produced by Christ Jesus during his teaching life. He was very tall and slight, remarkably mild and earnest. He wore a long garment so white and shining that it reminded me of the white raiment that surrounded the Lord at his transfiguration (Abraham's white garment was quite dingy compared with it). He wore also a girdle with letters similar to that worn later by the Jewish priests, and like them his head was covered with a small gothic miter during the sacrifice. His hair was shining yellow like long glittering strands of silk, and his countenance was luminous.

Upon Melchizedek's arrival, he found the king of Sodom already with Abraham in his tent, and around were numbers of people with animals, sacks, and chests. All were very grave and solemn, full of reverence for Melchizedek, whose presence in-spired awe. He stepped to the altar, which was a kind of tabernacle, wherein he placed the chalice. There was also a recess in it, I think for the sacrifice.

Abraham had laid upon the altar the bones of Adam, which Noah had had in the ark. They now prayed before them that God would fulfill the Promise made to Adam of a future messiah. Melchizedek spread upon the altar first a red cover, which he had brought with him, and over that a white transparent one. The ceremony reminded me of the holy mass. I saw him elevate the bread and wine, offer, bless, and break. He reached to Abraham the chalice used afterward at the Last Supper in order that he might drink. All the rest of those present drank from the little vessels that were handed around by Abraham and the most distinguished personages. The bread too was passed around in morsels larger than those given at holy communion in the early times. I saw these morsels shining. They had only been blessed, not consecrated. The angels cannot consecrate. All who partook of the food were filled with new life and drawn nearer to God.

Melchizedek gave bread and wine to Abraham, the former more luminous than that received by the others. Abraham derived from it great strength and such energy of faith that later on, at the command of God, he did not hesitate to sacrifice his child of promise. He prophesied in these words: "This is not what Moses upon Sinai gives the Levites," or "In this we differ from what Moses gives the Levites." I know not whether Abraham also offered the sacrifice of bread and wine, but I do know that the chalice from which he drank was the same used by Jesus at the Institution of the Most Holy Sacrament.

When Melchizedek at the sacrifice of bread and wine blessed Abraham, he at the same time ordained him a priest. He spoke over him the words: "The Lord said to my Lord, sit thou at my right hand. Thou art a priest forever according to the Order of Melchizedek. The Lord hath sworn, and he will not repent." He laid his hands upon Abraham, and Abraham gave him tithes. I understood the deep signification of Abraham's giving tithes after his ordination. But the reason of its importance I no longer recollect.

I saw also that David, when composing this psalm, had a vision of Abraham's ordination by Melchizedek, and that he repeated the last words prophetically. The words, "Sit thou at my right hand," have a peculiar signification. When the eternal generation of the Son from the Father was shown me in vision, I saw the Son issuing from the right side of the Father as a luminous form surrounded by a triangle, as the eye of God is depicted, and in the upper corner I saw the Holy Spirit. But it is inexpressible!

I saw that Eve came from the right side of Adam, that the patriarchs carried the Blessing in their right side, and that they placed the children to whom they delivered it upon their right. Jesus received the stroke of the lance in his right side, and the Church came forth from the same right side. When we enter the Church, we go into the right side of Jesus, and we are in him united to his heavenly Father.

I think that Melchizedek's mission upon earth was ended with this sacrifice and the ordination of Abraham, for after that I saw him no more. The chalice with the six cups he delivered to Abraham.

In vision, Anne Catherine said that the sacrifice of Melchizedek took place on a hill in the valley of Jehosaphat, though she could no longer place it more precisely. At the time, he already possessed the chalice of the Last Supper, which she could see. Abraham must already have known something of the sacrifice, and also that it would soon come, for he built the most beautiful and sturdy altar I had yet seen, over which was spread a canopy of foliage, like a tent. Within was a small sacramental structure, in which Melchizedek placed the chalice.

The vessels from which Melchizedek gave Abraham to drink were made of a precious stone. There was also a recess in it, I think for the sacrifice. Abraham had also brought with him a flock. The chalice must have been in the keeping of the sons of Noah. A goodly number of Noah's descendents were to be found later in Babylon, used mostly as slaves and much oppressed—and it seems to me the chalice was with them. Melchizedek led them out from this bondage, and took the chalice with him.

When Melchizedek raised up Jerusalem, some of these people worked with him, as did also some uncivilized natives of the region who lived in caves and huts. He built at three locations, laying extraordinarily deep and secure foundations. He also built something, and planted on all sides grapes and grain. He also built something where later stood the house of the Last Supper and the Temple, and as well on the side of Mount Golgotha.

It seems to me that the chalice then remained with Abraham. It was fabricated of some natural material, through which I have looked, and was in thickness like a bell—I could not tell whether grown or cast, but not hammered. The smaller vessels were worked from silver.

On an occasion when I saw Jesus take hold of the chalice, I beheld a side-picture, or image. Abraham was kneeling before an altar, and in the distance, in what seemed martial array, moved all manner of people, animals, camels. Then entered and came to Abraham's side a figure holding the selfsame chalice I had seen in Jesus's hand. He placed it on the altar before which Abraham was kneeling, and I beheld a brilliance, like wings, on his shoulders. I do not think he had wings in truth, but that they appeared that I might know him to be an angel. This was indeed the first time I ever saw wings on an angel. Behind Abraham's altar rose three clouds of smoke, the middle one high and vertical, the other two lower. Then I beheld two lines of ancestors, both leading to Jesus. Among them were David and Solomon. This was the stem of Jesus. Above Abraham I beheld Melchizedek and the names of kings—and with this, I then returned [in my vision] to Jesus holding the chalice.

The ancestors of Jesus received the Germ of the Blessing for the incarnation of God; but Jesus Christ himself *is* the sacrament of the New Covenant, the fruit, the fulfillment of that Blessing, to unite men again to God. When Jeremiah at the time of the Babylonian captivity hid the Ark of the Covenant and other precious objects on Mount Sinai, the Mystery, the Holy Thing, was no longer in it; only its coverings were buried by him with the Ark. He knew, however, what it had contained and how holy it was. He wanted, therefore, to speak of it publicly and of the abomination of treating it irreverently. But Malachi restrained him and took charge of the Holy Thing himself. Through him it fell into the hands of the Essenes, and afterward was placed by a priest in the second Ark of the Covenant. Malachi was, like Melchizedek, an angel, one sent by God. I saw him not as an ordinary man. Like Melchizedek, he had the appearance of a man, differing from him only inasmuch as was suited to his time.

Abraham Receives the Sacrament of the Old Covenant

ABRAHAM sat in front of his tent under a large tree by the roadside [see page 137]. He was in prayer. He often sat thus, waiting to show hospitality to travelers. As he prayed he raised his eyes to heaven and saw, as in a sunbeam, an apparition from God that announced to him the coming of the three whitish men. He arose and sacrificed a lamb on the altar, before which I saw him kneeling in ecstasy begging for the redemption of humankind. The altar stood to the right of the large tree, in a tent open above. Further on was a second tent, in which were kept vessels and other utensils for sacrifice. It was to this last that Abraham generally retired when superintending the shepherds who dwelt around here. Still further on, and on the opposite side of the road, was the tent of Sarah and her household. The women folk always lived apart.

Abraham's sacrifice was almost accomplished when he beheld the three angels appear on the highroad. On they came in their girded garments, one after another, an even distance between them. Abraham hurried out to meet them. Bowing low before God he saluted them and led them to the tent of the altar. Here they let down their garments and commanded Abraham to kneel.

I saw the wonderful things that now happened to Abraham through the ministry of the angels. He was in ecstasy, and all the actions were rapid, as is usual in such states. I heard the first angel announce to Abraham as he knelt that God would bring forth from his posterity a sinless, an immaculate, maiden who, while remaining an inviolate Virgin, should be the mother of the Redeemer, and that he was now to receive what Adam had lost through sin. Then the angel offered him a shining morsel and made him drink a luminous fluid from a small cup shaped in this way:

After that he blessed him, drawing his right hand in a straight line down from Abraham's forehead, then from the right and the left shoulder respectively down under the breast, where the three lines of the blessing united:

Then with both hands the angel held something like a little luminous cloud toward Abraham's breast and then enter into the region of Abraham's loins, growing smaller and taking the shape of something like a bean of light. I felt as if he were receiving the blessed sacrament.

The second angel told Abraham that he should, before his death, impart the mystery of this Blessing to Sarah's firstborn in the same way he had himself received it. He informed him also that his future grandson, Jacob, would be father to twelve sons, from whom twelve tribes should spring. The angel told him also that this Blessing would be withdrawn from Jacob, but that after Jacob had become a nation it would be restored and placed in the Ark of the Covenant as a Holy Thing belonging to that whole nation. It should be theirs for as long as they gave themselves to prayer. The angel explained to Abraham that on account of the wickedness of men the Mystery would be removed from the Ark and confided to the patriarchs, and that at last it would be given over to a man [Joachim] who would be the father of the promised Virgin. I heard also that, by six prophetesses and through star pictures, it had been made known to the pagans also that the redemption of the world should be accomplished through a Virgin. All this was made known to Abraham in vision, and he saw the Virgin appear in the heavens, an angel hovering at her right and touching her lips with a branch. From the mantle of the Virgin issued the Church.

The third angel foretold to Abraham the birth of Isaac. I saw Abraham so full of joy over the promised Holy Virgin and the vision he had had of her that he gave no thought to Isaac, and I think that this same Promise made the command he subsequently received to sacrifice Isaac easier for him.

After these holy communications I saw how, when Abraham awoke from ecstasy, he led the angels under the tree and placed stools around it. The angels sat down and he washed their feet. Then Abraham hurried to Sarah's tent to tell her to prepare a meal for his guests. This she did and, veiling herself, carried it halfway to them. The meal over, Abraham accompanied the angels a short distance on their journey. It was then that Sarah heard them speak to him of the birth of a son—she had approached them behind the enclosure of the tent. She laughed.[1] I saw numbers of

[1] Genesis 18:12.

Abraham and the Three Angels

Abraham's Counsel to Sarah

doves tame as hens before the tents. The meal had consisted of the same kind of birds, round loaves, and honey. I saw Abraham escorting the angels at their departure and heard him supplicating for Sodom.

Abraham, at his departure from Chaldea, had already received the mystery of the Blessing from an angel, but it was given him then in a veiled manner, and was more like a pledge of the fulfillment of the Promise that he should be the father of an innumerable people. Now, however, the Mystery was resuscitated in him by the angels, and he was enlightened upon it.[1]

The Place Where Abraham
Received the Blessing from the Angels

IN answer to a question regarding the location where Abraham received the angelic Blessing, Anne Catherine outlined the following map on her bed sheet, describing each feature according to the letter-key given below.

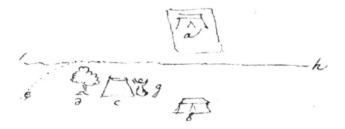

(a) The main living tent of Abraham and Sarah, with a cover stretched over it.

(b) A tent that housed various implements Abraham employed when offering sacrifice.

(c) The tent, open at the top, where the altar was kept, offering a view through its door-flap onto the main street.

---

[1] On one occasion Anne Catherine said that she thought Abraham had received the Blessing already in Mesopotamia, that the angel had only awoken the Blessing in the sacred grove of Mamre, as it was then that Sarah was ripe to conceive Isaac.

(d) A great tree.

(e) The path by which the angels approached.

(f) The main road.

Sarah was to be found [primarily] in the living tent (a), and Abraham—when not occupied with the many shepherds in the surrounding fields—mostly in tent (b).

The women lived somewhat to themselves. Abraham stored all that was necessary to offer sacrifice in tent (b), which he would then carry to tent (c) when he built the sacrificial fire on the altar, at which times he would kneel, or else sit praying upon his knees before the opening to the tent, his back turned to the street outside. At the moment he saw the angels approaching along path (e), Abraham's offering was nearly at an end.

At that point Abraham ran to the angels, who went with him to the place (g), and then commanded that he kneel, whereupon the Promise—as has been said before—was in him fulfilled. After he had returned to himself, he led the angels beneath the tree (d) and washed their feet, after which he ran to Sarah in tent (a), who then prepared a meal, which she brought, after veiling herself, half the way to them. Then she retired behind the tent-partitions. But she remained watchful, and when she heard the angels announce that she was to bear a son, she laughed. This took place as the angels removed, accompanied by Abraham, from (g) toward (h). I saw many doves, who were as tame as chickens running around. They [the assembly of angels and Abraham] ate honey and bread [with cooked doves].

✝ ✝ ✝ ✝ ✝

ON Wednesday, June 15, AD 29, I saw Jesus in Dothaim, a scattered little place northeast of Sepphoris, in which there was a synagogue. The inhabitants were not bad, though much neglected. Abraham had once owned fields there for his cattle intended for offerings. Joseph and his brethren used to guard their flocks in this same region, and it was here that the former was sold.

On Sunday, August 28, AD 29, some Nazarites invited Jesus to eat with them. During the course of the meal, some of them spoke about circumcision. Jesus said something to this effect, that the law of circumcision had a reason for its existence which would soon be taken away, when the people of God would come forth no longer according to the flesh from the family of Abraham, but spiritually from the baptism of the Holy Spirit.

In connection with a conversation between Jesus and Eliud the Essene on Tuesday, September 26, AD 29, Anne Catherine reports: Jesus related the fact of his having taken flesh of the blessed Germ of which God had deprived Adam before his fall. That blessed Germ, by means of which all Israel should have become worthy of Him, had descended through many generations. He explained how his coming had been so often retarded, how some of the chosen vessels had become unworthy. I saw all this as a reality. I saw all the ancestors of Jesus and how the ancient patriarchs at their death gave over the Blessing sacramentally to the firstborn. I saw that the morsel and the drink out of the holy cup, which Abraham had received from the angel along with the promise of a son, Isaac, were a symbol of the most holy sacrament of the New Covenant, and that their invigorating power was due to the flesh and blood of the future messiah. I saw the ancestors of Jesus receiving this sacrament in order to contribute to the Incarnation of God; and I saw that Jesus, of the flesh and blood received from his forefathers, instituted a most august sacrament for the uniting of humankind with God.

Jesus spoke much to Eliud also of the sanctity of Anne and Joachim and of the supernatural conception of Mary under the golden gate. He told him that not by Joseph had he been conceived, but from Mary according to the flesh; that she had been conceived of that pure Blessing which had been taken from Adam before the fall, which through Abraham had descended until it was possessed by Joseph in Egypt, after whose death it had been deposited in the Ark of the Covenant, and thence withdrawn to be handed over to Joachim and Anne.

DURING the period when John left the desert, the country around Salem and Ainon was, as it were, free, possessing a kind of privilege established by custom, by virtue of which the inhabitants dared not drive anyone from its borders. John had built his hut at Ainon on the old foundations of what was once a large building, but which had fallen to ruins and was now covered with moss and overgrown by weeds. Here and there arose a hut. These ruins were the former foundations of the tent castle of Melchizedek.

Of this place in particular I have had visions, all kinds of scenes belonging to early times, but I can now recall only this, that Abraham once had a vision here. He pulled two stones in position, one as an altar, and upon the other he knelt. I saw the vision that was shown to him—a City of God like the heavenly Jerusalem and streams of water falling from the same. He was commanded to pray more for the coming of the City of God. The water streaming from the City spread around on all sides. Abraham had this vision about five years before Melchizedek built his tent castle on the same spot. This castle was more properly a tent surrounded by galleries and flights of steps similar to Mensor's castle in Arabia. The foundation alone was solid, being of stone. I think that even in John's time the four corners where the principal stakes once stood were still to be seen. On this foundation, which now looked like a mount overgrown with vegetation, John had built a little reed hut. The tent castle in Melchizedek's time was a public halting place for travelers, a kind of charming resting place by the pleasant waters.

Perhaps Melchizedek, whom I have always seen as the leader and counselor of the wandering races and nations, built his castle here in order to be able to instruct and entertain them. But even in his time it had some reference to baptism. It was also the place from which he set out to his building near Jerusalem, to Abraham, and elsewhere. Here it was also that he assembled the various races and peoples whom he afterward separated and settled in different districts.

On Monday, October 3, AD 29, accompanied by some others, Jesus left Ainon and, returning by another route, arrived toward evening at a city built on both sides of a mountain, through which ran a rugged valley full of deep ravines. Both mountain and city bore the name of Ephraim, or Ephron. The mountain faced straight toward Gaza. Jesus had come through the country of Hebron. At some distance from the road that he traveled could be seen a ruined city with a tower still standing, whose name sounded like Malaga. About an hour's distance from this place was the grove Mamre whither the angels bore to Abraham the promise of a son, Isaac; also the double cave that Abraham bought from Ephren, the Hethite, and which afterward formed his tomb. The field that witnessed David's combat with Goliath was not far off.

Regarding Wednesday, October 12, AD 29, Anne Catherine reports that Abraham had once dwelt at Succoth with his nurse Maraha, and had owned fields in three different localities. Even here he had begun to share with Lot. It was here that Melchizedek first appeared to Abraham in the same way as did the angels. Melchizedek commanded him a threefold sacrifice of doves, long-beaked birds, and other animals, promising to come again and offer bread and wine in sacrifice. He told him what was going to happen to Sodom and to Lot, and pointed out to him several graces for which he should pray. Melchizedek at that time had no longer an earthly abode at Salem. The remote ancestors of Abraham, who had been settled in Hazezon by Melchizedek, had become very degenerate, and Abraham was, by a second exercise of God's mercy, led to the promised land. Melchizedek had been in these parts long before the Jordan existed. He had measured off and determined everything. He often came and went, and sometimes he was accompanied by a couple of men, who appeared to be slaves.

And regarding Thursday, August 24, AD 30, we read that the field in which lay Joseph's well was in the neighborhood of Gennabris, and Jesus took the occasion to refer to a somewhat similar struggle recorded in the Old Testament. Abraham had given far more land to Lot than the latter had demanded. After relating this fact, Jesus asked what had become of Lot's posterity and whether Abraham had not recovered full propriety. Ought we not to imitate Abraham? Was not the kingdom promised to him and did he not obtain it? This earthly kingdom however was merely a symbol of the kingdom of God, and Lot's struggle against Abraham was typical of the struggle of man with man. But, like Abraham, man should aim at acquiring the kingdom of God. Jesus quoted the text of holy scripture in which the strife alluded to is recorded, and continued to talk of it and of the kingdom before all the harvest laborers.

On Monday, August 28, AD 30, Jesus arrived in the little city of Abel-Mehola, where in earlier times Rebecca had run a school for orphans, who, according to Anne Catherine, learned of God's having made choice of the race of Abraham, to make of his descendants his chosen people from whom the Redeemer was to be born. For this purpose he had called Abraham from the land of Ur and had set him apart from the infidel races. They were told of God's sending "white men" to Abraham, that is, men who appeared white and luminous. These men had confided to Abraham the mystery of God's Blessing, owing to which his posterity was to be great above all the nations of the earth. The transmitting of that mystery they referred to only in general terms, as of a Blessing from which redemption should spring. They were told also about Melchizedek's being a "white man" like those sent to Abraham, of his sacrifice of bread and wine, and of his blessing Abraham. The chastisement inflicted by God upon Sodom and Gomorrah formed a part of the instruction given.

On Saturday, October 14, AD 30, Jesus came to the wooded valley to the east of Aruma, which extended from east to west in the direction of Sichar and northward to the mountain northeast of Shechem. To the east of this mountain, which rose in the midst of the plain of Shechem, was the little wood known as the grove of Mamre. It was there that Abraham had first pitched his tent, there also that God appeared to him and made to him the promise of a numerous posterity. A large tree stood nearby. Its bark was not so rough as that of the oak and it bore flowers and fruit at the same time. The latter were used for the knobs of pilgrim staffs. It was near this tree that the Lord appeared.

On the morning of Wednesday, January 10, AD 31, with his disciples, Jesus came to the forest of Mamre, a valley full of oaks, beeches, and nut trees that stood far apart. At the edge of the forest was the vast cave Machpelah, in which Abraham, Sarah, Jacob, Isaac, and others of the patriarchs were entombed. The cave was a double one like two cellars. Some of the tombs were hewn out in the projecting rocks, while others were formed in the rocky wall. This grotto is still held in great veneration. A flower garden and place for instruction guard its entrance. The rock was thickly clothed with vines, and higher up grain was raised. Jesus entered the grotto with the disciples, and several of the tombs were opened. They first put off their shoes outside the entrance, walked in barefoot, and stood in reverential silence around Abraham's tomb. Some of the skeletons were fallen to dust, but that of Abraham lay on its couch in a state of preservation. From it they unrolled a brown cover woven of camel's-hair cords thick as a man's finger. Jesus taught here. He spoke of Abraham, of the Promise and its fulfillment.

On Tuesday, May 1 AD 30, Jesus was traveling with some pagan philosophers. During the whole journey, he taught these savants, sometimes walking, sometimes tarrying in some lovely spot. He instructed them upon the absolute corruption of humankind before the deluge, of the preservation of Noah, of the new growth of evil, of the vocation of Abraham, and of God's guidance of his race down to the time in which the promised consoler was to come forth from it.

The pagans asked Jesus for explanations of all kinds, and brought forward many great names of ancient gods and heroes, telling him of their benevolent deeds.[1] The philosophers made mention also of one of the most ancient of the wise kings who had come from the mountainous regions beyond India. He was called Jamshid. With a golden dagger received from God he had divided off many lands, peopled them, and shed blessing everywhere. They asked Jesus about him and the many wonders which they related of him. Jesus answered that Jamshid, who had been a leader of the people, was a man naturally wise and intelligent in the things of sense. Upon the dispersion of men at the time of the building of the tower of Babel, he had put himself at the head of a tribe and taken possession of lands according to certain regulations. He had fallen less deeply into evil because the race to which he belonged was itself less corrupt. Jesus recalled to them also the

---

[1] The balance of this section largely repeats what was given earlier above in "Melchizedek" and "The Tower of Babel," but is provided here for ease of reference more particularly in connection with the story of Abraham.

fables that had been written in connection with him, and showed them that he was a false companion-picture, a false type of Melchizedek, the priest and king. Jesus told them to fix their attention on the latter and upon the descendants of Abraham, for as the stream of nations moved along, God had sent Melchizedek to the best families, that he might guide them, unite them, and make ready for them countries and dwellings in order to preserve them in their purity and, according to their worthiness or unworthiness, either hasten or retard the fulfillment of the Promise. Who Melchizedek was, he left to themselves to determine; but of him this much was true, he was an ancient type of the then far-off, but now so near grace of the Promise, and the sacrifice of bread and wine which he had offered would be fulfilled and perfected, and would endure till the end of the world.

The large chalice used at the Last Supper once belonged to Abraham. Melchizedek brought it from the land of Semiramis, where it was lying neglected, to the land of Canaan, when he began to mark off settlements on the site afterward occupied by Jerusalem. He had used it at the sacrifice of bread and wine offered in Abraham's presence, and he afterward gave it to him. This same chalice was even in Noah's possession. It stood in the upper part of the ark. Moses also had it in his keeping. The cup was massive like a bell. It looked as if it had been shaped by nature, not formed by art. I have seen clear through it. Jesus alone knew of what it was made.

Some Words on Christ's Descent into Hell in Connection with Abraham

WHEN Jesus with a loud cry gave up his most holy soul, I saw it as a luminous figure surrounded by angels, among them Gabriel, penetrating the earth at the foot of the holy cross. I saw his divinity united with his soul, while at the same time it remained united to his body hanging on the cross. I cannot express how this was. I saw the place whither the soul of Jesus went. It seemed to be divided into three parts. It was like three worlds, and I had a feeling that it was round, and that each one of those places was a kind of locality, a sphere separated from the others. Just in front of limbo there was a bright, cheerful tract of country clothed in verdure. It is into this that I always see the souls released from purgatory entering before being conducted to heaven. The limbo in which were the souls awaiting redemption was encompassed by a gray, foggy atmosphere, and divided into further circles.

The Savior—resplendent and conducted in triumph by angels—pressed on between two of these circles. The one on the left contained the souls of the leaders of the people down to Abraham, that on the right the souls from Abraham to John the Baptist. Jesus went on between these two circles. They knew him not, but all were filled with joy and ardent desire. It was as if this place of anxious, distressed longing was suddenly enlarged. The Redeemer passed through them like a refreshing breeze, like light, like dew, quickly—like the sighing of the wind.

The Lord passed quickly between these two circles to a dimly lighted place in which were our first parents, Adam and Eve. He addressed them, and they adored him in unspeakable rapture. The procession of the Lord, accompanied by the first human beings, now turned to the left, to the limbo of the leaders of God's people before the time of Abraham. This was a species of purgatory, for here and there were evil spirits, who in manifold ways worried and distressed some of those souls. The angels knocked and demanded admittance. There was an entrance, because there was a *going in*; a gate, because there was an *unlocking*; and a *knocking*, because the one that was coming had to be announced. It seemed to me that I heard the angel call out: "Open the gates! Open the doors!"

Jesus entered in triumph, while the wicked spirits retired, crying out: "What hast thou to do with us? What dost thou want here? Art thou now going to crucify us?" and so on. The angels bound them and drove them before them. The souls in this place had only a vague idea of Jesus, they knew him only slightly; but when he told them clearly who he was, they broke forth into songs of praise and thanksgiving. And now the soul of the Lord turned to the circle on the right, to limbo proper. There he met the soul of the good thief [Dismas] going under the escort of angels into Abraham's bosom, while the bad thief [Gesmas], encompassed by demons, was being dragged down into hell. The soul of Jesus addressed some words to both and then, accompanied by a multitude of angels, of the redeemed, and by those demons that were driven out of the first circle, went likewise into the bosom of Abraham.

Jacob
(Isaac, Rebeccah, Esau, Laban, Rachel)

W E know that wonderful things happened to Abraham through the ministry of the three angels.[1] He heard the first angel announce that God would bring forth from his posterity a sinless, an immaculate maiden who, while remaining an inviolate Virgin, should be the mother of the Redeemer, and that he was now to receive what Adam had lost through sin. The first angel then offered Abraham a shining morsel and made him drink a luminous fluid out of a little cup, and after blessing him in the way earlier described, with both hands held something like a little luminous cloud toward Abraham's breast, which entered into him, as if he were receiving the blessed sacrament.

The second angel told Abraham that he should, before his death, impart the mystery of this Blessing to Sarah's firstborn (Isaac) in the same way that he had himself received it. The second angel informed Abraham also that his future grandson, Jacob, would be the father of twelve sons, from whom twelve tribes should spring. This angel told him also that this Blessing would be withdrawn from Jacob, but that after Jacob had become a nation, it should be again restored and placed in the Ark of the Covenant as a Holy Thing belonging to the whole nation, and should be theirs for as long as they gave themselves to prayer. The angel explained to Abraham that, on account of the wickedness of men, the Mystery would be removed from the Ark and confided to the patriarchs, and that at last it would be given over to a man [Joachim] who would be the father of the promised Virgin. All this was made known to Abraham in vision, and he saw

---

[1] See the foregoing "Abraham," of which a resume is here repeated in the event the reader is presently focused primarily on the story of Jacob.

the Virgin appear in the heavens, an angel hovering at her right and touching her lips with a branch. From the mantle of the Virgin issued the Church.

The third angel foretold to Abraham the birth of Isaac. I saw Abraham so full of joy over the promised Holy Virgin and the vision he had had of her, that he gave no thought to Isaac, and I think that this same Promise made the command he subsequently received to sacrifice Isaac easier for him.

NOW Rebecca [wife of Isaac and mother of Jacob and Esau] knew that Esau had no share in the divine Mystery. He was dull, rough, and slothful; Jacob very active and shrewd, more like his mother. Isaac, however, was partial to Esau as his firstborn. Esau was often away from home hunting. Rebecca pondered frequently how she could procure the birthright, the Blessing, for Jacob, and she taught him how to go about buying it. The mess of pottage for which Esau sold it was composed of vegetables, meat, and green leaves like lettuce. Esau came home tired from the chase. Jacob coaxed him, and received the surrender of the birthright.

Isaac was at this time very old and blind. He feared he would soon die, and consequently was anxious to give his Blessing over to Esau. Rebecca, who knew that Jacob should and must have it, could not persuade Isaac to give it to him. She was on that account very much afflicted, and went around quite anxious. When she found that Isaac would no longer be withheld from imparting the Blessing, and that he called to him Esau, who was in the neighborhood, she laid her plans. She told Jacob to hide when his brother came in, that he might not be seen. Isaac ordered Esau to go bring him something of his hunting. Then Rebecca sent Jacob to get a kid from the flock, and hardly was Esau gone when the dish for Isaac was prepared.

Esau's best clothes, which Rebecca now put upon Jacob, consisted of a jacket very like Jacob's own, only stiffer and embroidered on the breast in colors. Esau's arms and breast were covered with thick, black hair like wool, his skin being like the skin of an animal; therefore Rebecca wrapped a part of the kid's skin around Jacob's arms and put a piece upon his breast where the jacket lay open. This jacket differed from the one usually worn only by the amount of work upon it. It was slit at the sides, and passed over the head by a hole that was bound with soft, brownish leather. The side slits were fastened together with leather strings, and when a girdle was worn over it the fullness around the breast served as a pocket. No garment was worn under this jacket, which was sleeveless and left the breast bare. The headgear and apron worn with the jacket were brownish, or gray.

I saw Isaac feeling Jacob's breast and hands where Esau was full of hair. I saw that he wavered a little, troubled and doubting. But then came the thought that, notwithstanding his doubts, it was certainly Esau and that God willed him to have the Blessing. And so he made over to Jacob that Blessing which he had received from Abraham, and Abraham from the angel. He had, with Rebecca's assistance, previously prepared something mystical connected with it; that is, a drink in a cup.

The other children of the patriarchs knew not of it. Only the one that received the Blessing knew of the mystery which, however, still remained to him—as to us the blessed sacrament—a mystery. The cup was rather flat on one side. It was transparent and shone like mother-of-pearl. It was filled with something red, something like blood, and I felt that it was Isaac's blood. Rebecca had helped to prepare it.

When Isaac blessed Jacob, they were alone. Jacob bared his breast and stood before his father. Isaac drew the hand with which he gave the Blessing from Jacob's forehead straight down to the abdomen, from the right shoulder to the same point, and the same from the left shoulder. Then he laid his right hand on Jacob's head and his left upon the pit of his stomach, and Jacob drank the contents of the little cup. And now it seemed as if Isaac delivered to him all things, all power, all strength, while with both hands he took, as it were, Something out of his own person and placed it in that of Jacob. I felt that this Something was his own strength, that it was the Blessing. All this time Isaac was praying aloud. While giving over the Blessing, Isaac sat erect on his couch; he became animated and rays of light streamed from him. When Isaac drew his hand down in giving the Blessing, Jacob held both of his open and half-raised, as the priest does at the *Dominus vobiscum*; but

The Mess of Pottage

Jacob Deceives Isaac

when the father merely prayed, Jacob kept them crossed on his breast. When Isaac delivered the Blessing to Jacob, the latter received it and crossed his hands under his breast like one who is holding something. At the close of the ceremony Isaac laid his hands upon Jacob's head and upon the region of the stomach, and then Jacob received the cup out of which he had drunk.

When the imparting of the Blessing had been accomplished, I saw Isaac swooning, either from exertion or from having actually given over and parted with his strength. But Jacob was radiant, quickened, full of life and strength. And now came Esau from the hunt.

When Isaac discovered that the Blessing had been transferred to the wrong one, he had no regret, recognizing it to be God's will. But Esau was mad with rage, he tore his hair. Still, in his fury there seemed to be more envy of Jacob than grief for the lost Blessing.

Both Esau and Jacob were full-grown men, over forty years old at the time of the transfer of the Blessing. Esau already had two wives who were not much liked by his parents. When Rebecca saw Esau's rage, she sent Jacob away secretly to her brother Laban. I saw his departure. He wore a jacket that reached to the waist, an apron as far as the knees, sandals on his feet, and a band wrapped round his head. In his hand was a shepherd's staff, a small sack containing bread hung from his shoulder, and under his arm was a flask. This was all he took with him. I saw him hurrying off, followed by the tears of his mother. Isaac had blessed him a second time and commanded him to go to Laban, and to take a wife in his new home. Isaac and Rebecca had much to endure from Esau. Rebecca especially had much sorrow.

I saw Jacob on his journey to Mesopotamia lying asleep on the spot where Bethel afterward stood. The sun had set. Jacob lay stretched on his back, a stone under his head, his staff resting on his arm. Then I saw the ladder that Jacob beheld in his dream, and which in the bible is described as "standing upon the earth, and the top thereof touching heaven." I saw this ladder rising up to heaven from Jacob where he lay upon the earth. It was like a living genealogical tree of his posterity. I saw below on the earth— just as those genealogical trees are represented—a green trunk as if growing out of the sleeping Jacob. It divided into three branches that arose in the form of a triangular pyramid whose apex reached the heavens. The three branches were connected by other smaller ones that formed a three-sided pyramidal ladder. I saw this ladder surrounded by numerous apparitions. I saw on it Jacob's descendants, one above another; they formed the ancestry of Jesus according to the flesh. They often crossed over from side to side, stepping past and even before one another. Some stood back and others from the opposite side stepped before them, according as the Germ of the sacred humanity was clouded by sin and then again purified by continence until at last the pure flower, the Holy Virgin in whom God willed to become man, appeared on the highest point of the ladder touching the heavens. I saw heaven open above her and disclose the splendor of God. God spoke thence to Jacob.

I saw Jacob awake the next morning. First he built a round foundation of stone on which he laid a flat stone, then he raised upon this the stone he had placed under his head the preceding night. Lastly he made a fire and offered something in sacrifice; he also poured something into the fire on the stone. He knelt while praying and I think he kindled the fire as the three kings did, that is, by friction.

I saw Jacob in many other places also, at Bethel for instance, as he journeyed to Laban, staff in hand. I saw him at Ainon, where he had been before and where he repaired a cistern that later on became John's fountain of baptism.[1] I saw him also pass over the Jabbok. I saw him even at that early period praying at the spot Mahanaim. He begged almighty God to protect him and also to keep his clothes from becoming shabby, lest on his arrival in Mesopotamia his uncle Laban on account of his miserable appearance might not acknowledge him. Then he beheld two troops of angels hovering on either side of him like two armies. This was shown him as a sign of God's protection over him, and of the

---

[1] Elsewhere, Anne Catherine says: "Before Jacob lived in Abel-Mehola, at a distance from his home, on account of Esau's wrath, he dwelt with his herds for a time by Ainon, where to the east upon a hill remained the foundations of Melchizedek's tent castle, as also the cistern of what later became the baptismal pool, which Jacob at that time restored."

power that should be given unto him. The fulfillment of this vision he saw on his return journey.

Then I saw him going further eastward, along the south side of the river Jabbok, and passing a night on the spot where he afterward wrestled with the angel. Here too he had a vision.

On Jacob's return from Mesopotamia, his encampment lay east of the encampment of the subsequent Jabesh-Gilead. I saw Laban, his father-in-law, following him in pursuit of his lost idols. Laban overtook him, and words ran high between them on the score of the idols, for Jacob did not know that Rachel had secretly brought them with her.[1] When Rachel saw that her father, who had been searching the whole encampment for his lost treasures, would soon reach her tent, she took the stolen idols and hid them under a heap of fodder not far from her own tent. The idols were metal dolls, about two and a half arms long, in swaddling clothes. The heaps of fodder were on a slope of the valley south of the Jabbok, and were for the use of the camels. Rachel muffled herself up and sat down on one of them, as if she were sick and had retired for a while. Many other women sat like her on the other heaps. On a similar, though somewhat larger, straw heap I have seen the leprous Job sitting. That on which Rachel sat was of the size of a full harvest wagon. They brought quantities of fodder with them on the camels, and on the way often laid in fresh supplies of it. These idols had long been a subject of scandal to Rachel, and she carried them off merely to disengage her father from them.[2]

Jacob had sent messengers to Esau, of whom he was in dread. They returned with the news that Esau was at hand with four hundred men. Then Jacob divided his whole train into two bands. His best flocks he divided into several and sent them on to Esau. He then led his followers to Mahanaim, where he had for the second time the vision he had seen on his setting out—that is, of the angelic armies. He said: "With my staff did I set out, but I am now

---

[1] Brentano notes here that Anne Catherine proceeded to describe this scene exactly as in scripture.

[2] She told what followed then almost completely, and determined the place where the memorial stones had been erected after Jacob's reconciliation with Laban, southwest from the valley of the Fidelity of the Camel on the heights.

richer by two armies." He now understood the signification of that first vision.

When his whole train had crossed the Jabbok, Jacob sent his wives and children over by night, and remained alone. Then he ordered his tent to be erected on the spot where, on his journey from Palestine, he had seen the face of God. He wanted to pray there by night. He ordered his tent to be closed on all sides and bade his servants retire to some distance. Then I saw him crying with his whole heart to God. He laid all things before Him, especially his great anxiety with regard to Esau. The tent was open above, that he might better send forth his prayers to heaven.

Then I saw him wrestling with the angel. It took place within a vision.[1] Jacob arose and prayed. Then there descended from above a light in which was a great luminous figure, which began to wrestle with Jacob as if wanting to push him out of the tent. They wrestled here and there, up and down, in all directions through the tent. The apparition acted as if wanting to draw Jacob toward all regions of the world, but Jacob always faced about to the center of the tent. This struggle prefigured the fact that Israel, though pressed on all sides, should not be forced from Palestine.

But when Jacob once again faced to the middle of the tent, the angel grasped him by the hip. I saw this take place when Jacob, who was wrestling in vision, wanted to cast himself upon his couch, or sink back upon it. When the angel touched Jacob's hip and at the same time did what he wanted to do, he said to the latter, who was holding him fast: "Let me go, for the dawn is breaking!" Then Jacob ceased struggling and awoke from his vision.

Seeing the angel of God still standing before him, he cried: "No, I will not let thee go until thou bless me!" He felt the need of God's Blessing, for he knew that strength had departed from him and that Esau was at hand. Then spoke the angel: "How art thou called?" (This belonged to the Blessing: Abram also at his Blessing was renamed Abraham). He answered: "Jacob." Then said the angel: "Thou shalt be called Israel, for thou hast wrestled

---

[1] "From this I came to see how something that occurs in a dream can at the same time represent a real event—for even as he slept I saw that in his sleep Jacob arose and prayed."

with God and men, and hast not been vanquished." Then Jacob said: "How art thou called?" And the angel answered: "Why dost thou ask me how I am called?"—which words signified: "Dost thou not know me? Hast thou not already learned who I am?" And Jacob knelt before him, and received the Blessing. The angel blessed him as Abraham had been blessed by God, as Abraham had imparted the Blessing to Isaac, and Isaac to Jacob; that is, in three lines, as already described.

The Blessing was especially to ensure peace and perseverance. And now the angel vanished. Jacob saw that the dawn was breaking and he named the place Phanuel. He ordered his tent to be taken down, and he crossed the Jabbok to his family. And now the sun arose upon him. He limped on the right side, for he had there been deprived of strength.

When Esau turned off, Jacob went with all his family, his servants, and his herds, to Mahanaim and took possession of the country from Succoth to the hill Ainon. He dwelt ten years at Ainon. He afterward extended his settlement westward from Ainon and over the Jordan to Salem. His tents reached to where Shechem dwelt, for there he bought a field.

The patriarchs Abraham, Isaac, and Jacob had more strength in their right side than in their left; it was not however noticeable, for their garments were wide and full. There was in their right side a certain fullness like a swelling. It was the Holy Thing, the Blessing, the Mystery. It was luminous, in shape like a bean, and it contained a Germ, which Abraham had received from God, Yes, the Blessing rested in the right side of Abraham, and signified the most holy, and a numerous progeny. The sacrament of the Old Covenant was in consequence the sacrament of holy procreation in Abraham. That made him so holy, and for that reason his servant Eliezer, when he swore him to bring to his son Isaac a wife from Mesopotamia, was required to lay his hand under the hip of Abraham, and to swear in the belief in the messiah promised in the Blessing given to the patriarchs.[1]

---

[1] See "Lineage of Abraham's Trusted Servant to Alpheus & Mary Cleophas" below (pp. 163–65).

Because in vision I experience things more as visible forms than as heard words, I always saw the Holy Thing of the Blessing as being within the patriarchs—for it signified a holy fruitfulness in the likeness of a shining plant seed rather like a bean of light with an illuminated kernel. On occasions when the firstborn were blessed, I saw this Holy Thing pass into the firstborns, and it was on this account that they rose to prominence over all others.[1]

But Jacob received it instead of Esau, because his mother Rebecca knew he was the one destined for it. It was in defense of this Blessing that Jacob wrestled with the angel, who by virtue of contact with Jacob—and according to God's will—removed the Blessing from Jacob. In this, Jacob was in no way wounded, for it was through the hand of God that it was taken from him, even as it had been through the hand of God that Abraham received it—as had Isaac also from Abraham, and Jacob from Isaac.[2] It was as though a twig were broken off an ennobled branch, thereby weakening it. So was it in this case also, for the patriarchs appeared to have a strength in their right hips under their wide garments, but Jacob now seemed weakened, as though the Blessing had to some degree vanished, or dried up.

After the removal of the Blessing, Jacob no longer lived so securely, so immediately under God's protection. While he possessed the Blessing, he was like one strengthened by a sacrament; afterward, however, he felt himself humiliated; he was careworn and he experienced more troubles. He was conscious of the Blessing's having been withdrawn from him, therefore he would not let the angel go until he had received from him a New Blessing.

At the time of the conception of his youngest son, Benjamin—at whose birth his mother Rachel would die—Jacob no longer possessed Abraham's Blessing, from which would spring the line of the messiah—but he had another, a New Blessing.[3]

---

[1] It was the firstborn who received it from the father, hence the prerogatives of primogeniture. CB

[2] Anne Catherine remarked that Isaac lived for twenty-six years after Jacob's return [from Laban].

[3] It is quite striking how at a later time nearly the entire line of Benjamin would be extinguished on account of a misdeed. CB

Jacob's son Joseph—later on, when in the prison of Pharaoh in Egypt—received that same Blessing from an angel.

It seems to me that one time I saw Joseph imprisoned by Pharaoh, at a time when he was in his greatest need, receive the Blessing again—brought to him in his sleep by an angel, who placed it in his breast.[1]

When Jacob was traveling to Bethel, his sons and their wives were obliged to give over to him any stolen good or idols in their possession, and all their gold. All this he buried beneath an oak tree close by Sichem, partly because he did not wish to carry unjustly obtained goods, partly also because he wished to have with him no treasure that might tempt robbers to fall upon his party. To this end the women gave over also their ear ornaments, which consisted of long strands hanging together from a ring, some of these extending all the way to the breast, where they were then fastened.[2]

When Jacob bestowed the many-colored coat upon his son Joseph, he gave over to him also some of the bones of Adam, without telling him, however, what they were. Jacob gave them to Joseph as a precious talisman, for he knew well that his brothers did not love him. Joseph carried the bones on his breast in a little leathern bag rounded on top. When his brothers sold him, they took from him only the colored coat and his customary outer garment, but left the band and a sort of scapular on his breast, beneath which he had hung the little bag.[3]

One day, after the evening meal, Anne Catherine remarked that

---

[1] "At this time I saw Jacob's daughter Dinah walking around there with her maids and conversing out of curiosity with the Shechemites. I saw Shechem caressing her, for which reason her maids went away, and he took her with him into the city. This was the cause of great sorrow to Dinah, while bloodshed and slaughter accrued from it to the Shechemites. Shechem at that time was not yet a great city. It was built of large, square stones and had only one gate."

[2] Anne Catherine described these as similar to the pendants on the necks of peasant women from the region of Münster, from which little crucifixes hang, though these are somewhat broader (she called them "plates").

[3] When Jacob came to Egypt, he asked Joseph about the treasure, and then revealed to him that it contained the bones of Adam.

during the previous night she had seen Jacob struggling with the angel, and that the latter had broken something out of his right side, so that a cavity remained in the space where it had been—and that thereby was the Mystery taken from him. But unfortunately she could no longer recall for what reason it was taken from him. The angel had also told Jacob the reason, but Jacob had not understood it, and for that reason had wrestled with the angel. It had something to do with showing preference to certain children, and with a white garment of innocence that he (Jacob) wanted to give one child.

Rectification Concerning the Star of Jacob

ANNE *Catherine saw Jacob's ladder as terminating in the star into which she had looked, wherein she beheld God reflected, and above which stood the heavenly Jerusalem. Various other forms gradually took shape upon the ladder, the first being that of the Virgin holding the scales. The great tower with many gates below was the house of bread—that is, Bethlehem—into which entered the Virgin with the Child, and so forth. (It would be a mistake then to think there had also been a house upon the ladder.)*

Anne Catherine was unfortunately quite inconvenienced at this time, and so forgot other pertinent details. However, she quite correctly located on an enlarged version of a map (made by Klöden) the valleys of Palestine and the river Jabbok. She also correctly pinpointed the locations of Ramoth, Jabesch, and Gerasa, although they were not marked on the map. She positioned Mahanaim somewhat farther to the east and Succoth on the southern bank, but Phanuel south of Jabesch. She was totally at home with this map and quite accurately traced upon it Jacob's movements through the region. She was familiar with even the smaller valleys and what had transpired within them—all with an extraordinary certitude. Here is what she had to say:

When, much later, Jacob went into Egypt to Joseph, he pursued the same route through the wilderness by which later on Moses journeyed to the promised land. Jacob knew that he would see Joseph again; he always had a presentiment of this in his heart. He had, even on this journey to Mesopotamia, at the place upon which he erected the altar (not where he saw the ladder), a vision of his future sons, one of whom he saw, in the region where Joseph was sold, sink from sight and like a star rise again in the south. He exclaimed therefore, when they brought him the blood-stained coat (the foregoing circumstance, by then almost forgotten, recurring to him), "I shall weep for Joseph until I find him again." Jacob had, through Reuben, made many inquiries as to whom Joseph had married, but had not yet been entirely enlightened on the point that Joseph's wife was his own niece.[1] Rueben and Potiphar were old acquaintances. Owing to the influence of the former, the latter received circumcision and served the God of Jacob.

Jacob dwelt about a day's journey distant from Joseph. When he fell sick, Joseph drove in a chariot to see him. Jacob questioned him closely about Asenath, and when he heard of the sign on her person he exclaimed: "She is flesh of thy flesh. She is bone of thy bone!" and he revealed to Joseph who she was. Joseph was so deeply affected that he almost lost consciousness. On his return home he told his wife and both shed tears to their heart's content over the news.

Some time after, Jacob grew worse, and Joseph was again by his side. Jacob put his feet from the couch to the floor and Joseph had to lay his hand under his father's hip and swear to bury him in Canaan. While Joseph swore, Jacob adored the Blessing hidden in him, for he knew that Joseph had received from an angel the Blessing that had been withdrawn from himself.[2] Joseph bore this Blessing in his right side until death.[3] Three months after his visit, Jacob died. Both Jews and Egyptians celebrated his obsequies and sounded his praises, for he was greatly loved.

---

[1] As is described in more detail in "Joseph and Asenath" in *Mysteries of the Old Testament*, Joseph's wife was the daughter of Jacob's only daughter, Dinah.

[2] A later note by Brentano: "Hebrews 11:21: '[Jacob] leaning on the tip of his scepter.' Referring to I Moses 47:31 in the Septuagint: 'The scepter will neither be taken from Judah, nor from the host that come from his loins.' I wonder if these words have a relevance here?"

[3] Even after death it lay enclosed in his body until the night before the departure of the Israelites, when Moses took possession of it and placed it in the Ark of the Covenant, together with the remains of Joseph, as the Sacred Thing of the chosen people. See "Moses" in *Mysteries of the Old Testament*.

ON Tuesday, October 17, AD 30, Jesus healed the sick in Thanat-Shiloh and then went into the fields, which were being harvested. There he taught, again referring to unnecessary and exaggerated concern for the cares of life (Matthew 6:25–34). He went next day into the harvest field and cured many whom he found there. Some people brought out from the city baskets of provisions, and a great entertainment was spread in one of the tabernacles that still remained standing. Jesus afterward delivered the long discourse in which he spoke against unnecessary and extravagant care for the preservation of life, as has been mentioned. He brought forward the example of the lilies. They do not spin, and yet they are clothed more beautifully than Solomon in all his glory. Jesus said many beautiful things to the same effect of the different animals and objects around. Such instructions were much needed by the people of this place, for they were extraordinarily covetous and greedy for gain in trade and agriculture. There were no Pharisees here. The people were rather coarse but very proud of their descent from Abraham. The sons of Abraham, however, whom the patriarch had settled here, had soon degenerated. They intermarried with the Shechemites, and when Jacob returned to that region the law of circumcision was already forgotten. Jacob had intended to fix his residence there but was deterred from doing so by (his daughter) Dinah's seduction.[1] He knew the children of Abraham who dwelt in those parts, and sent them presents. Dinah had gone to take a walk by the well of Salem. Some of the people in the fields, those to whom her father had sent presents, invited her to visit them. She was accompanied by her maids, but leaving them, she ventured alone into the fields, desirous of gratifying her curiosity. It was then that the Shechemite saw and ensnared her.

On November 17, AD 30, upon entering a synagogue and approaching the pulpit, Jesus found it occupied by one who was reading aloud. The latter, however, at once arose and yielded his place to Jesus, who immediately took the roll of scriptures and

---

[1] See "Dinah" (*not* "Dinah the Samaritan Woman") in *People of the New Testament V.*

began to teach upon the passages referring to Jacob's being called to account by Laban, his struggle with the angel, his reconciliation with Esau, and the seduction of Dinah.

Lineage of Abraham's Trusted Servant to Alpheus & Mary Cleophas

ANNE *Catherine had often remarked that a relic contained in an old cross she had brought with her from the convent was a bone fragment from Mary Cleophas. On one occasion the pilgrim removed this relic from the cross and brought it to her wrapped under a different guise. She was quite awake when she took hold of it, though perhaps somewhat distracted, and said shortly thereafter that it seemed very old to her, older even than Jesus and those who had traveled in his company. After a troubled night, she said again that the bone was from Mary Cleophas, and that the latter had appeared to her more clearly than before, saying: "This is bone of my bone." Then she related what follows, regarding some of which she had spoken on other occasions also:*

At the beginning of their marriage Anne and Joachim conceived a daughter [Mary Heli]. Anne however regarded this child as "after the flesh," feeling that in her conception she had perhaps done wrong. And so, leaving the child with her parents, she and Joachim removed to Nazareth to live a secluded life of repentance. At the age of around sixteen, this first daughter married a man named Cleophas, who served as Joachim's head shepherd, and gave birth in due course to a daughter, Mary Cleophas.

About four years after the birth of her granddaughter (Mary Cleophas) Anne gave birth to the Virgin Mary, whom this very night I saw as a child playing together with her elder niece.

During the years when the Virgin Mary was living in the Temple, Mary Cleophas married one of her father Joachim's shepherds, a man no longer young, perhaps in his thirties. He was called Alpheus, and in vision this past night I witnessed their wedding.[1] It took place in a small place not far from Nazareth, where the bridegroom's mother and father lived. The wedding was as

---

[1] That is, Joachim and Anne's eldest daughter, Mary Heli, had married her father's head shepherd (Cleophas), and later their daughter Mary Cleophas in

large an affair as was the wedding at Cana. At the wedding I saw Alpheus's father, a small, bent old man with a long beard, who came from the region of Bethlehem. He was called Solana, or Solama, or perhaps Sulama—I am no longer sure which.

My gaze then moved from Solana back toward Bethlehem, where he occupied nearby a small property that had originally formed part of the manor and estate where Joseph's parents had lived, and then I saw the family line of Alpheus's father stretching far back to Abraham's time. I saw how this family line always progressed alongside that of the humanity of Jesus, ramifying in side branches, and then smaller branches, but never in such a way that the first lineage directly connected with the second; rather, the second lineage always accompanied the first in a subordinate relationship of service.

Then I beheld Abraham kneeling beside a hut set on a hill; and on the further side of that same hill I saw the huts of the progenitor of the second lineage. He was Abraham's most true and trusted servant, and was also kneeling at prayer. Abraham was praying for Sodom and Lot, and just then I perceived above Sodom a great, impending danger. The man of whom I speak was the father of Eliezer, the servant whom Abraham called to lay his hand under his thigh and swear to bring back from his fatherland a wife for his son Isaac.[1]

This lineage [descending from the father of Elieazer] would ever after accompany that of Jesus, but in a secondary or tertiary manner—present always in the same fields and gardens as the stem of Jesus, but in a subservient, dependent role. That the progenitor of this lineage remained so true to Abraham that, even when the latter's brother Lot abandoned him, he remained by Abraham's side, came to expression again—as though in reward or recompense—in that Alpheus remained true in the same way to [his grandfather-in-law] Joachim as had his ancient forbear [the

---

turn married one among her grandfather's shepherds (Alpheus), over whom her father presided as overseer. See "Mary Heli" in *People of the New Testament V.*

[1] Genesis 24:1–5.

father of Eliezer] to Abraham. Thus did the sons of Alpheus—now in a spiritual sense—come to stand by Jesus also as messengers and shepherds, as overseers of his flocks.[1]

The pilgrim here adds: There is no way adequately to describe the wondrous manner in which Anne Catherine perceived such lines of descent and family connections branching out through millennia. All that can be said is that she beheld all pictorially, in the form of a tree whose essential stem was always the true one. She knew exactly which branch it was that represented the above-described relationship to Abraham. She even lay her finger on the coverlet of her bed, outlining just where this lineage branched off—and as she did so spoke further thereof while shifting her finger to yet another place, believing (because such is how she experienced it) that others must see it also. When others do not understand her explanations, which are often very difficult to follow, she readily becomes distressed, saying that their failure to understand must be on account of their not being priests.

---

[1] The natural sons of Alpheus and Mary Cleophas were the apostles Judas Thaddeus, Simon the Zealot, and James the Less. There were also two daughters: Susanna Alpheus and Mary Alpheus. In addition, when Alpheus wed Mary Cleophas, he brought to their union from a prior marriage another son, who likewise became an apostle—Levi, later called Matthew. It may be added that after Alpheus died, Mary Cleophas twice remarried, first to Sabbas, to whom she bore the disciple Joseph Barsabbas; then to Jonah (a brother of Peter's wife), who brought to the marriage a son named Parmenas, who became a disciple also. To Mary Cleophas and Jonah was then born Simon Justus, who became the second bishop of Jerusalem.

Jacob's Body is Taken to Egypt

Printed in Great Britain
by Amazon